HARRY G. JOHNSON

THE TWO-SECTOR MODEL OF
GENERAL EQUILIBRIUM

Yrjö Waldemar Jahnsson, 1877–1936, was Professor of Economics at the Institute of Technology, Helsinki. In 1954, his wife Hilma Jahnsson established, in accordance with her husband's wishes, a foundation.

The specific purpose of the Yrjö Jahnsson Foundation is to promote economic research in Finland. To this end the Foundation supports the work of individual scholars and institutions by awarding them scholarships and grants. It also invites internationally renowned economists to Finland to give courses of lectures which are then published in this series.

YRJÖ JAHNSSON LECTURES
Kenneth J. Arrow
Aspects of the Theory of Risk-Bearing

Assar Lindbeck
*Monetary-Fiscal Analysis and
General Equilibrium*

Books by Harry G. Johnson
*The Overloaded Economy
International Trade & Economic Growth
Money, Trade & Economic Growth
Canada in a Changing World Economy
The Canadian Quandary
The World Economy at the Crossroads
Economic Policies towards Less Developed Countries
Essays in Monetary Economics
Aspects of the Theory of Tariffs*

YRJÖ JAHNSSON LECTURES

The Two-Sector Model
of
General Equilibrium

HARRY G. JOHNSON

Professor of Economics, The London School of Economics and
Political Science, and the University of Chicago

LONDON
GEORGE ALLEN & UNWIN LTD

First published in 1971

ISBN 0 04 330182 7 *cased*
0 04 330183 5 *paper*

Printed in Great Britain
in 10 point Baskerville type
by Alden & Mowbray Ltd at the Alden Press, Oxford

PREFACE

It was a great privilege to me to be invited to deliver the Yrjö Jahnsson lectures in Finland in September 1970, and thus to meet Finnish colleagues and their students. I used the occasion to bring together materials I have been developing, very largely as teaching aids and short-cuts for graduate students, over the past twenty-odd years. The techniques of geometrical general-equilibrium analysis originate in my primary field of international trade theory, but I have found them extremely useful in a course in the theory of distribution I have been offering at the University of Chicago since 1965, and the lectures draw primarily on that material, only a part of which has previously been published, and then only in rather obscure places.

I have taken advantage of the publication of the lectures to add three short appendices that may assist students: mathematical notes on the one-sector model; an early note applying the techniques to the analysis of the incidence of excise taxes; and some notes of recent vintage applying the two-sector model to the problem of public goods.

I am grateful to the Yrjö Jahnsson Foundation both for the stimulus provided by their invitation to give the lectures, and for the efficiency and hospitality of their arrangements during my visit to Helsinki and Tampere. I am particularly grateful to Mr Seppo Hieta, Managing Director of the Foundation, for his services as a companion and cicerone. I am also glad to have had the opportunity to meet that wonderful lady, Mrs Hilma Jahnsson, who established the Yrjö Jahnsson Foundation in her husband's memory and who is personally primarily responsible for having made it a powerful force for the promotion of Finnish economic research.

The London School of Economics and   HARRY G. JOHNSON
Political Science   *November 1970*

CONTENTS

I

The Two-sector Model of Production and Distribution

The Yrjö Jahnsson lectures have already, in their relatively short existence, established a well-deserved reputation for solid contributions to the literature of positive scientific economics, as contrasted with the more transient concern with current issues of economic policy characteristic of some comparably distinguished lecture series. For my contribution to the series, I have chosen to develop and expand the two-sector model of general equilibrium. My purpose is not so much to produce new theoretical propositions, as to synthesize techniques of analysis that have been developing in various fields, notably international trade theory and the theory of public finance, and apply them to various traditional problems of general economic theory, notably in the theory of distribution. This may not seem a very ambitious undertaking. But in my view one of the important responsibilities of the academic scholar, in his capacity as teacher, is to render himself gradually obsolete by simplifying and synthesizing his hard-won knowledge so as to make it readily available to later generations and thus enable them to make further progress more rapidly.

Nor may some find my virtually exclusive reliance on geometry appealing, since it is widely assumed that to be elegant and impressive theory has to be as mathematical as possible. But mathematical economic theory has two major limitations, as compared with geometrical analysis. First, as a tool for exploring theoretical problems, it is frequently more cumbersome and less flexible than geometry, which can achieve significant results using only qualitative restrictions on the shapes of relevant behaviour functions and can explore problems in the large as well as in the small. Second, and more important, geometry lends itself far more readily than mathematical analysis to the communication of economic analysis to masses of students (though this advantage may be eroding as students in general become more numerate). The vast increase in economic literacy that has occurred in this century owes much to two simple but powerful geometrical techniques of analysis: the 'Marshallian cross' of the demand and the supply curve which brought micro-economics within the range of first-year university and now high-school students, and the 'Hicksian cross' of the investment-savings (IS) and liquidity preference – money supply (LM) equilibrium relations, which was largely responsible for the rapid propagation of the Keynesian Revolution among young professional economists and which has similarly made macro-economics teachable at the pre-university level. The geometrical analysis I shall present is, of course, more complex than these, but will I hope prove similarly useful as an instrument for teaching and exploration.

Before I proceed to the construction of the two-sector general equilibrium model, which will occupy the rest of this lecture, I should like as a background to summarize briefly two familiar one-sector models of production and distribution, both focused on the problem of the functional distribution of income – the Ricardian model and the Hicksian model.

The Ricardian model of distribution may be thought of as a one-sector model, in the sense that Ricardo attempted to deduce the general laws of distribution from what happens in the agricultural sector. Virtually all the problems and difficulties of Ricardo's model stem from the fact that this cannot be done;

but the basic or 'ideal' Ricardian model is still interesting and important as a source of contemporary ideas on and problems of distribution theory. In that model, land is fixed in overall quantity, but output can be increased by cultivating existing farm-land more intensively or extending the margin of cultivation. The land is worked by labour; but labour needs to be supported over the crop season by a stock of agricultural produce – the 'wages fund' provided by capitalists in return for profits. Profits are the difference between the marginal product of labour and the wages that must be paid for it. In the short run, wages are determined competitively by the number of workers divided into the wages fund; in the long run wages are fixed by the level of subsistence, through population increase or decrease. At any point of (long-run) time, the size of the wages fund determines the size of the labour force, the marginal product of labour, and the rate of profit – and hence the incentive to accumulate more capital. In the long run, accumulation is brought to a halt by the fall in the rate of profit, necessitated by the diminishing marginal productivity of labour on the fixed stock of land, to the minimum level acceptable to the capitalists.

The Ricardian model is illustrated in the accompanying Figure 1. The wages fund at a point of time is $O\overline{W}.OL_0$, with the rectangular hyperbola DD representing the short-run relation between the wage rate and the size of the labour force. For simplicity, it is assumed that the latter is appropriate to the subsistence wage, at OL_0. For this labour force, average product is OQ_0, marginal product is OP_0, rent is the rectangle $Q_0P_0.OL_0$, profits are the rectangle $P_0\overline{W}.OL_0$ (the profit rate being $P_0\overline{W}/O\overline{W}$), and wages are the wages fund $O\overline{W}.OL_0$. If capitalists accumulate capital as long as the profit rate exceeds some minimum rate p, the economy will approach the long-run stationary equilibrium position with labour force OL_s, average product of labour OQ_s, and marginal product of labour $P_s = (1+p)\overline{W}$. Labour's share in total output must rise, and the combined share of land and capital fall; but, contrary to the impression given by the diagram, though the absolute amount of rent must rise, it is not inevitable that the relative share of rent rise at the expense of the combined relative shares of wages and profits.

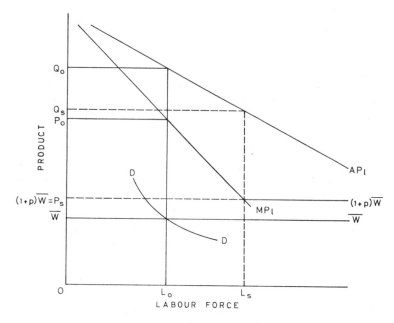

FIGURE I

This depends (to anticipate) on whether the elasticity of substitution between land and labour in agricultural production is less than or greater than unity. It might also be noted that the diagram gives a slightly misleading picture of the dynamics of accumulation: if capital is accumulating the labour force must be growing at the same rate (in the longer run), and this implies a wage rate higher enough than the long-run static-population

12

subsistence wage $\overline{W}$ to support the larger-sized families required by population growth.[1]

The model developed by J. R. Hicks in his *Theory of Wages*, and explored in great detail in the 1930s, makes use of an aggregate constant-returns to scale production function in which labour and capital enter as arguments. The assumption that capital can be treated as an original factor of production was rightly disputed in a review of Hicks' book by Gerald Shove which led Hicks to refuse reprinting of it for a long period; and this assumption has continued to be a key point of criticism of the 'neoclassical' theory of production and distribution by the post second war Cambridge School led by Joan Robinson and Nicholas Kaldor. I shall, however, ignore this problem for the time being, a procedure that can be rationalized by identifying 'capital' with a stock of perfectly malleable equipment used in the production process, in combination with labour.

The essential contributions of the Hicks model were the introduction of the elasticity of substitution as the parameter governing the effect of factor growth on relative income shares and influencing its effect on absolute incomes, and a classification of types of technical change according to their effect on relative income shares. The model is illustrated in Figure 2, where the axes measure endowments of capital and labour and the curves are isoquants of the aggregate production function. With given stocks C_0 of capital and L_0 of labour, competition maximizes output at the point P_0, in the process establishing a price ratio for labour in terms of capital represented by the slope of M_0M_0'; C_0M_0 represents the value of labour's contribution to output in terms of capital, i.e. the amount of labour OL_0 valued at its price in terms of capital (the slope of M_0M_0'), C_0M_0/C_0O, the ratio of labour's income to capital's income, is the negative of the slope of M_0M_0' (the price of labour

---

[1] I am indebted for this point to an unpublished paper by David Levy of the University of Chicago.

in terms of capital), divided by the slope of OR_0 (the ratio of capital to labour used in production), or the reciprocal of the ratio of capital to labour multiplied by the relative price of capital.

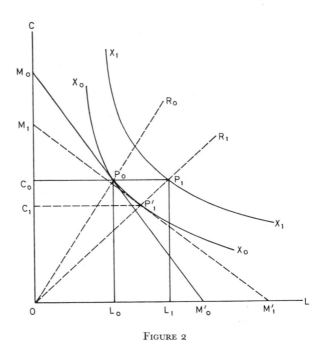

FIGURE 2

An increase in the stock of one factor (labour in the diagram, from L_0 to L_1) must increase the absolute income of the other factor, owing to the assumptions of constant returns to scale and of diminishing marginal rate of substitution between the factors in production. The relative share of the augmented factor may increase or decrease, and in the latter eventuality its absolute share may even decrease. Because of constant returns to scale, the behaviour of relative shares may be analysed in terms of the shift along the original isoquant from P_0 to P_1', the ratio of labour's to capital's share changing from $C_0 M_0 / O C_0$ to $M_1 C_1 / O C_1$.

These ratios as already mentioned are the reciprocals of the product of the relevant capital-labour ratio and relative price of capital; and labour's relative share will rise, be constant, or fall according as the fall in the capital-labour ratio between P_0 and P_1' is greater, equal to, or less than the associated rise in the relative price of capital. The technically given elasticity of the capital-labour ratio with respect to the relative price of capital is defined as the elasticity of substitution; hence labour's relative share rises, is constant, or falls, according as the elasticity of substitution is numerically greater than, equal to, or less than unity.

The effects of technical progress can be represented by drawing a new isoquant with a higher product index through the original endowment point P_0. If the new isoquant has the same slope there as the old one, technical progress has raised the marginal products of the two factors in the same proportion as the increase in total output, relative shares are unchanged, and the innovation is classed as 'neutral'. If the new curve cuts the old from north-east to south-west, capital's marginal product has risen more than labour's, and the innovation is classified as 'labour-saving'; and conversely for a 'capital-saving' invention. Sufficiently biased innovation will reduce the absolute as well as the relative income share of the factor it saves.

Apart from the objections that may be raised – for quite different reasons – against their treatment of the nature of capital, both the idealized Ricardian model and the Hicksian model of distribution suffer from the restrictive characteristic of one-sector models, the elimination of demand factors, which makes the functional distribution of income a mechanistic consequence of the available technology and factor supplies.

This limitation is the essence of the Cambridge School's attack on neo-classical production and distribution theory. But the defect is easily remedied by constructing a two-sector model, in which preferences and demands for the two products influence the general equilibrium outcome that determines factor prices and distribution.

For the purpose of constructing such a model, it is assumed (as in the Hicks analysis) that endowments of the two factors, capital and labour, are given, and that problems of the nature of capital can be evaded by identifying capital as a malleable physical stock of productive equipment. Production of each of the two goods is assumed to require the use of both factors in a constant-returns-to-scale production function; commodity X is assumed to be relatively capital-intensive as compared with commodity Y, in the sense that at any factor-price ratio common to the two industries the cost-minimizing capital-labour ratio is higher in X than in Y. For purposes of introducing demand considerations into the determination of general equilibrium, it is assumed that each of the two factors is owned exclusively by one group of the population, and that each group can be treated as having a single aggregate preference function. This assumption, while in accordance with a long tradition in economic theory going back through Marx to Ricardo, is not essential, and it would be easy enough to work with the alternative assumption of two groups with unequal shares in ownership of the two factors.

To avoid problems with corner solutions, each group is assumed always to demand some of both goods, at all relative commodity prices.

With these assumptions, construction of the model can proceed in terms of either of two geometrical techniques: the Lerner-Pearce diagram and the Edgeworth-Bowley contract box diagram. The latter is the more traditional, the former the newer and probably less familiar outside the field of international trade theory. Since both have their advantages for particular problems, I shall develop each in turn. In each case the essential steps involve establishing a unique relationship between the production pattern, commodity prices, factor prices, and the distribution of income.

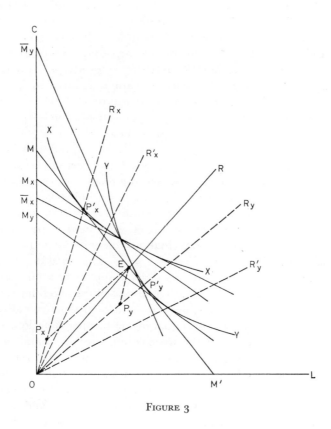

FIGURE 3

The Lerner-Pearce diagram, represented in Figure 3, exploits the fact that, owing to the assumption of constant returns to scale, the production function can be represented by a single isoquant (since relative and absolute factor marginal productivities depend only on the ratio in which factors are combined in production). In the diagram, XX and YY represent isoquants for arbitrarily chosen quantities of X and Y.

Given the isoquants, there will be one set of relative factor prices, represented by the common tangent MM' to the two isoquants, at which the two commodities will have equal costs of production; at these factor prices, the capital-labour ratios in their production will be OR_x and OR_y respectively. Now consider a slight rise in the price of capital relative to labour, represented by a counter-clockwise rotation of the common budget line; the optimal capital-labour ratios become OR_x' and OR_y', and the minimum cost of producing X in terms of capital become OM_x whereas the minimum cost of producing Y in terms of capital becomes OM_y. The relative cost of production of the capital-intensive good rises as the relative price of capital in terms of labour rises. There is thus a monotonic relation, given by the technology, between the relative costs (prices) of the goods and the relative factor prices, such that a rise in the relative (and absolute) marginal productivity of a factor is associated with a rise in the relative price of the good that uses it intensively. While the proof just given applies to a change in factor prices starting from an equal-cost-of-commodities situation, it is perfectly general, because units of product can always be re-defined to make costs equal in the starting situation.

The monotonic relation between commodity prices and factor prices is a perfectly general result of the assumed difference in factor intensities between the products, and holds so long as both are produced. The assumed fixity of factor endowments, however, sets limits to the range of commodity and factor prices the economy can in fact attain consistently with full employment of the factors of production. Assume that the country's endowment ratio of factors is OR (which must lie

18

between OR_x and OR_y if MM' is to be included in the feasible set of factor and commodity prices). At one extreme, the economy could employ its total factor endowment in producing X, implying a factor-price ratio represented by the slope of $\overline{M}_x\overline{M}_x{}'$ and a corresponding commodity-price ratio given by the ratio of OM_x to the y-intercept of a parallel tangent to the YY isoquant; at the other extreme the economy would specialize on producing Y, with a factor-price ratio given by the slope of $\overline{M}_y\overline{M}_y{}'$ and a correspondingly determined commodity price ratio (for diagrammatic simplicity $\overline{M}_x{}'$ and $\overline{M}_y{}'$ are not shown).

The foregoing implies that, given the factor endowment, there will be a unique relation between commodity prices, factor prices, and the production pattern – the allocation of factors between the industries. This allocation can be shown diagrammatically as follows. Let E, on our original common tangent to the two isoquants, represent the actual factor endowment of the economy. Then, given the optimal factor utilization ratios in the two industries determined by commodity and factor prices, the allocation of resources must be such that the amounts used in the two industries add up to the overall endowment. These allocations can be determined, on the principles of vector addition, by completing the parallelogram formed by the endowment point E and the optimal factor utilization ratios in the two industries: in the specific case of the budget line MM', the factor allocations will be as shown by P_x and P_y. Moreover, since with endowment E and the budget line MM' both XX and YY correspond to total national income, the shares of values of output of X and of Y in total national output are OP_x/OP'_x and P_xP_x'/OP_x' or P_yP_y'/OP_y' and OP_y/OP_y' respectively.

It is further evident that as the relative price of capital rises and of labour falls, P_x must shift to the north-east and P_y to the south-west, implying an increase in X production and a decrease in Y production. Since a higher relative price of capital implies also a higher relative cost (and price) of X, increased production of X involves a rise in relative cost of production in terms of Y foregone; hence, if we were to chart a transformation curve between X and Y for the economy, it would be concave to the origin.

Thus far, I have used the Lerner-Pearce technique to develop certain necessary relations among commodity prices, factor prices, and factor allocation on the production side of the economy. This gives a range of possible production and distribution situations, selection among which of the general equilibrium solution requires reference to demand conditions. Demand conditions are typically handled in terms of preference systems defined over commodities and subject to a budget constraint defined in terms of purchasing power over commodities, an approach which seems difficult to combine with an analysis of the production side in terms of factor utilization. However, the reconciliation can be easily accomplished by means of a technique developed by the Australian economist N. F. Laing.[1] The technique consists simply of recognizing that a budget constraint defined in terms of commodities at a given commodity-price ratio is also a constraint in terms of factors at the factor-price ratio corresponding to the commodity-price ratio, and that the goods demanded subject to that constraint can be decomposed into the factors required to produce them, via the optimal factor-utilization ratios corresponding to that factor-price ratio. In other words, given a bundle of commodities and the marginal rates of substitution (commodity-price ratios) at which the individual would consume that bundle, the bundle can be represented by a set of factor quantities and marginal rates of substitution (relative prices) among those factors. Thus the individual's preference function defined

[1] N. F. Laing, 'A Diagrammatic Approach to General Equilibrium Analysis', *Review of Economic Studies*, Vol. XXX (1), No. 82 (February 1963), pp. 43–55.

over commodities can be transformed into a preference system defined over factors.

This technique is applied in Figure 4, which reproduces the relevant parts of Figure 3. MM' is the common tangent to the

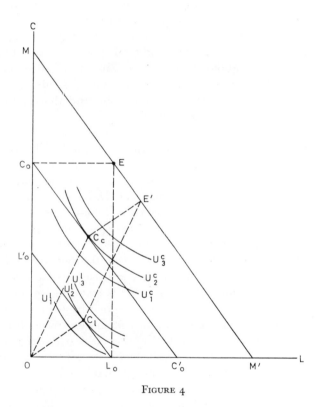

FIGURE 4

XX and YY isoquants (not shown) and E is the economy's factor endowment, consisting of OC_0 of capital and OL_0 of labour; C_0C_0' is the factor-command budget line of capital and L_0L_0' the factor-command budget line of labour. Capital's preference system in terms of factor command indicates maximum-utility consumption of factor services at the point C_c, and labour's preference system similarly defines consumption of factor services at the point C_L. Vector addition of the two consumption points indicates a total demand for factors at point E', reflecting an excess demand for labour and excess supply of capital, by comparison with the factor endowment E, to which must correspond an excess demand for Y and excess supply of X (respectively the labour-intensive and capital-intensive goods). To achieve equilibrium with the economy's given factor endowment, the price of labour must rise and that of capital must fall, until E' coincides with E.

There is, however, a possibility that a small rise in the relative price of labour and fall in the price of capital will move E' farther from and not nearer to E; and this possibility entails the possibility of multiple equilibria of which alternate ones will be unstable. A rise in the price of labour will rotate $C_0 C_0'$ clockwise about C_0 and $L_0 L_0'$ clockwise about L_0. In each case there will be a substitution effect increasing the demand for capital and reducing the demand for labour and hence working towards restoration of equilibrium. But the negative income effect on capital's consumption and positive income effect on labour's consumption will work towards restoring equilibrium only if labour has a higher marginal propensity to consume the services of capital than does capital; otherwise, the redistribution of income between the two groups will by itself tend to increase the excess supply of capital services rather than reduce it, and this effect may be strong enough to outweigh the stabilizing influence of the substitution effect. To put the point another way, it might be possible to arrive at consumption of factor services at endowment point E by raising rather than by lowering the price of capital services; and this would imply an unstable equilibrium possibility at E. Such an unstable equilibrium factor-price ratio, however, must always be bounded by at

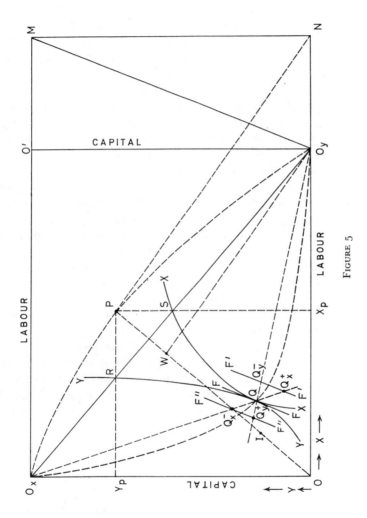

FIGURE 5

23

least one higher and one lower, and stable, equilibrium factor-price ratio.

The alternative approach to the development of the two-sector general equilibrium model utilizes the Edgeworth-Bowley contract-box diagram. This is depicted on the left-hand side of Figure 5. The vertical side of the box (OO_x) represents the economy's given endowment of capital, the horizontal side (OO_y) its given endowment of labour. Isoquants for X are sketched into the box with reference to the origin O_x, and for Y with reference to the origin O_y. The tangency points of the two sets of isoquants trace out the contract curve $O_x Q O_y$, which is the locus of efficient production, that is, of factor allocations which maximize the amount of one good that can be produced given the amount of the other to be produced. Such maximization requires equality of the ratios of marginal products of the two factors in the two industries. FF, the common tangent to isoquants for the two goods at the point Q, represents the equilibrium factor-price ratio at that point (i.e. for that combination of feasible outputs). Note that as Q moves along the contract curve in the direction of O_y, FF becomes less steep with reference to the horizontal because such a movement involves substitution of labour for capital along the isoquants for both production functions; that is, in effect, the production point travels north-east along the X isoquant and south-west along the Y isoquant. In other words, as production of X increases and of Y decreases, the relative price of labour falls and of capital rises; and, as seen earlier, this implies a rise in the relative price of X in terms of Y.

It would be possible at this point to take the relations among commodity prices, factor prices and income distribution, and the production pattern previously analysed in connection with the Lerner-Pearce diagram, as implicitly established from the box diagram, and to proceed with the analysis in terms of a transformation curve between the two commodities and a

24

corresponding income distribution function governing demand. But it is preferable theoretically to leave no potential loose ends, and to develop these concepts from the production contract box itself rather than by inference.

I begin by developing the production transformation curve between the two commodities from the contract curve.[1] Because of the assumption of constant returns to scale, the quantity of X produced can be measured for any production point in the contract box, by the distance cut off by the corresponding isoquant along any ray from the origin O_x; and similarly for production of Y with respect to any ray through the origin O_y. The diagonal of the box, O_xO_y, offers a convenient common ray to the two isoquant systems, for conducting the measurement. Thus the output of X at point Q can be measured by the distance O_xS cut off on O_xO_y by the X isoquant through Q, and similarly the output of Y at point Q can be measured by the distance O_yR cut off on O_xO_x by the Y isoquant through Q. The ratio O_xS/O_xO_y represents the proportion of the maximum possible output of X produced at Q; and the ratio O_yR/O_yO_x the proportion of the maximum possible output of Y produced at Q.

Moreover, by vertical projection the output of X can be measured along the horizontal axis OO_y, production being OX_p measured in units such that maximum possible production of X is OO_y, and by horizontal projection the output of Y can be measured along the vertical axis OO_x, production being OY_p measured in units such that the maximum possible production of Y is OO_x. These co-ordinates permit the plotting of point P, which shows the point on the production transformation curve corresponding to point Q on the contract curve, with reference to the origin O. Similar plotting of the corresponding point P

---

[1] This technique employed is due to K. M. Savosnick, 'The Box Diagram and the Production Possibility Curve', *Ekonomisk Tidskrift*, Vol. 60, No. 3 (September 1958), pp. 183–97.

as Q moves along the contract curve yields the complete transformation curve $O_x PO_y$, with reference to the origin O.

It is evident from the construction that every P must lie to the north-east of the diagonal $O_x O_y$; but this does not suffice to establish the usual assumption that the transformation curve under perfect competition is everywhere concave to the origin O. To prove this, hold factor prices constant at the price ratio embodied in FF and consider equal increases and decreases in production of X from Q to $Q_x{}^+$ and from Q to $Q_x{}^-$ respectively. At the given factor prices, production of Y would simultaneously decrease and increase by equal amounts, respectively from Q to $Q_y{}^-$ and from Q to $Q_y{}^+$ respectively. But maintenance of the initial factor price ratio is in each case inconsistent with factor market equilibrium, since it would involve an excess demand for capital and supply of labour for an increase in X production and vice versa for a decrease in X production. If factor prices are allowed to change to preserve factor market equilibrium, while X production is changed up and down by the same assumed equal amounts, the equilibrium production points must lie on the contract curve respectively somewhere right of $F'F'$ for the increase in X, and somewhere right of $F''F''$ for the decrease in X. This means that production of Y decreases when X increases by more, and increases when X decreases by less, than the equal decrease and increase that would occur if factor prices were held constant. Hence, as X increases from the quantity at $Q_x{}^-$ to the quantity at Q and then to the quantity at $Q_x{}^+$, a successively larger amount of Y production has to be sacrificed; and this proposition holds regardless of the magnitude of the equal successive changes in X production. Hence the transformation curve must be concave to the origin throughout.

I now develop the income distribution relationship. The factor-price ratio at point Q is given by the slope of FF. The value of capital in terms of labour can consequently be measured by drawing a line through O_y with the same slope as FF, to intersect O_xO' extended at M. O_xO' represents the income of labour in terms of labour, and $O'M$ the income of capital in terms of labour, their ratio representing the division of total income between the two factors. Drop MN perpendicular to OO_y produced, to transfer the distribution ratio to the horizontal axis. Then draw the lines OP and NP and draw O_yW parallel to NP to intersect OP at W. This divides OP into the segments OW and WP, with OW representing the share of labour and WP the share of capital in the total output represented by point P. Similarly, the division of income could be projected onto OP, with the income of capital being measured along OP from O, by drawing a line from O' parallel to MO_y, to intersect O_xO_y at some point, and then a line from this point parallel to OO_y to intersect OO_x, and finally a line from this point parallel to the line O_xP to determine the point I. Alternatively, I could be found by measuring a distance from O equal to the distance WP.

The points W and I are to be interpreted as reference points, and not as actual consumption points. Labour's income is actually a budget line through W, with reference to the origin O, with slope equal to that of the tangent to the transformation curve at P, and similarly capital's income is the same budget line but with reference to the origin P. Conversely, capital's income is the budget line through I parallel to the tangent at P with reference to the origin O, and labour's income is the same budget line with reference to the origin P.

The same procedure can be used to plot income distribution curves for labour and capital passing through W and I respectively. These curves will be reference curves, the location of the budget line being determined by the intersection of the line from the origin O to the relevant point on the transformation curve P with the reference curve. Since, as the output of X expands from zero to the maximum amount possible, the marginal product of capital must rise in terms of both products

27

and the marginal product of labour fall, the income distribution curves must have the property that as W moves south-east with P, successive budget lines for labour must lie inside their predecessors throughout their length; and conversely as I moves south-east with P, successive budget lines for capital must lie outside their predecessors throughout their length.

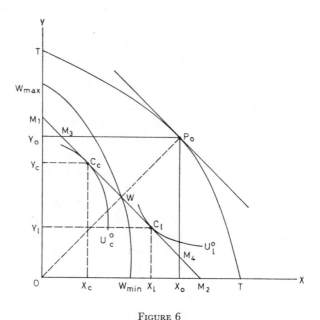

FIGURE 6

Given the method of derivation of the transformation curve and the income distribution functions the analysis of the general equilibrium determination of commodity and factor prices and the production pattern can now proceed without further reference to the contract box diagram. There are two alternative ways of proceeding, technically.

28

The first is to use a single income distribution function, with O and P as origins respectively for the indifference curve systems of the two groups of factor owners. This method is illustrated in Figure 6, where $W_{max}W_{min}$ is the income distribution curve for labour with reference to the origin O, the income of capital being represented by reference to the origin P_0, the relevant point on the transformation curve. With production at P_0, labour's budget line with reference to O is M_1M_2, while capital's budget line with reference to the origin P_0 is M_3M_4. Labour's indifference curves in conjunction with its budget line produce a consumption equilibrium point for labour at the point C_L; similarly capital's indifference curves in conjunction with its budget line produce a consumption equilibrium point for capital at the point C_c. Capital's consumption demand for Y is Y_0Y_c, and labour's OY_L, implying an excess of supply of Y over the demand of Y_cY_L; capital's consumption demand for X is X_0X_c, and labour's OX_L, implying an excess of demand for X over the supply of X_cX_L. To achieve equilibrium, the production pattern of the economy must shift towards production of more X and less Y, implying a rise in the price of capital and a fall in the price of labour, equilibrium being restored when, for the relevant point on the transformation curve, C_L and C_c coincide.

As was true on the approach of the Lerner-Pearce diagram, however, a shift of the production point south-east from P_0 along the transformation curve may accentuate rather than reduce the excess supply of Y and demand for X. Such a shift tends to be stabilizing in two ways: it increases the supply of X and reduces the supply of Y, and it exercises a substitution effect in the consumption of both groups of factor owners in favour of Y and against X, by raising the relative price of the latter as compared with the former. However, as production shifts towards more of X and less of Y, the income of the capitalist group in terms of purchasing power over both goods increases, and the income of the labour group in the same terms falls.

If capitalists have a higher marginal propensity to consume X (the capital-intensive good) than do workers, this shift in the distribution of income tends to increase the demand for X, the good whose relative price has risen, and this effect may be strong enough to offset the production and substitution effects just mentioned and increase the excess demand for commodity

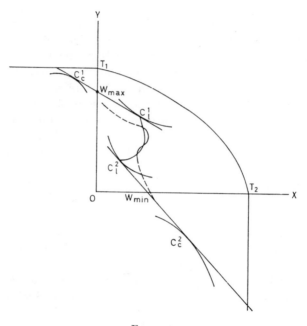

FIGURE 7

X. The possibility of such behaviour in turn implies the possibility of multiple equilibrium, though as before (and as usual) multiple equilibrium must be characterized by an odd number of alternatively stable and unstable equilibria.

The possibility of multiple equilibrium is illustrated in Figure

30

7, which reproduces some aspects of Figure 6. When the economy is specialized on production of Y, at T_1, capitalist consumption must be at a point like C_c^1, and labour consumption at a point like C_L^1, implying (on the assumption that both groups of factor owners always demand some of both goods) an excess supply of Y. Similarly, when the economy is specialized on production

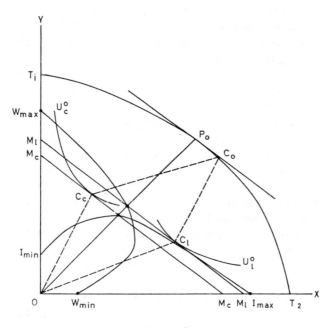

FIGURE 8

of X, at T_2, capitalist consumption must be at a point like C_c^2, and labour consumption at a point like C_L^2, implying an excess supply of X. Between C_c^1 and C_c^2 must run a locus of possible consumption points for capitalists, passing between C_L^1 and C_L^2, and between the latter two points must run a locus of possible consumption points for labour. These curves must intersect at least once, implying the existence of a stable equilibrium point for the economy as a whole. But they may intersect more than once – necessarily an odd number of times – as illustrated in the diagram, implying an alternation of stable and unstable possible equilibrium points.

The second possible approach is to employ two income distribution functions, one for labour and one for capital, with both sets of group indifference curves inserted in the diagram with reference to the origin O. This approach is illustrated in Figure 8, where $W_{max}W_{min}$ and $I_{min}I_{max}$ are the income distribution curves for labour and capital respectively. For production point P_0, labour's budget line is M_LM_L and capital's M_cM_c; capital's optimum consumption point is C_c, and labour's C_L. The total consumption demand of the community, derived by vector addition, is at C_0, implying an excess demand for X and supply of Y and requiring a rise in the relative prices of X and capital, a shift of production towards X, and a redistribution of income towards capital. As in the previous analysis of the Lerner-Pearce approach, there may be an income-redistribution effect of a rise in the price of X that increases the excess demand for it, if the substitution and production effects are weak and capital has a relatively strong marginal propensity to consume X; and this case again gives rise to the possibility of multiple equilibria.

This lecture has been devoted to the rather arid task of constructing a full general equilibrium two-sector model of the economy, bringing in income distribution and factor-owner preferences in addition to production conditions (technology and relative factor supplies) as determinants of the full equilibrium solution. The next lecture will apply the apparatus to the purpose for which such apparatus is intended, the analysis of the effects of exogenous and policy-induced changes on the characteristics of the general equilibrium solution of the system.

II

Applications of the Model

In my first lecture, I set up a complete two-sector model of general equilibrium, and derived the properties of its component functions. The purpose of such an exercise, however, is not primarily to demonstrate the existence of an equilibrium on reasonable general assumptions about tastes and technology and to explore its stability and uniqueness – though mathematical economists in particular have devoted considerable attention to these questions – but to apply the model to the investigation of economically relevant changes in the data of the system, including both exogenous changes and changes induced by policy. This is the purpose of the present lecture. Specifically, I shall apply the model first to some standard problems in the theory of income distribution, and then to the analysis of a variety of policies or institutional arrangements intended or expected to alter the distribution of incomes. In these applications, I shall employ extensively an analytical technique that I have found extremely useful for many such problems. It entails assuming that prices are held constant when a change occurs, examining the effects of the change on excess demands and supplies at those prices, and using the assumption of stability of equilibrium to predict the direction of price change required to restore equilibrium.

In the two one-sector models analysed briefly at the beginning of the first lecture, the Ricardian and the Hicksian, the analysis of distributional changes is simple, since demand conditions are excluded by assumption and the production side determines everything. In the Ricardian model, capital is the only variable factor whose rate of earnings can change in the longer run, capital accumulation must lower the profit rate, and technical improvement in agriculture must raise the profit rate except in the very long-run stationary state. In the Hicksian model, an increase in the quantity of a factor must lower the price per unit of that factor and raise that of the other, with the behaviour of relative shares being determined by the elasticity of substitution, while technical progress influences distribution according to its factor-saving bias. In the two-sector model, demand and substitution in consumption have to be taken into account, as must the fact that technical progress may occur in either of the two sectors, or in both at differential rates. There are, in fact, three basic types of change to be analysed; a shift of demand between the two commodities, accumulation of one of the factors, and technical progress in one of the industries.

Shifts of demand are the simplest to deal with. They must involve an increase in the quantity of one good demanded, and decrease in the quantity of the other demanded, by one or both groups of factor-owners, at given commodity prices and the corresponding distribution of income among the factors. The result is an excess demand for one commodity and excess supply of the other at the previously equilibrium-price ratio, requiring a change in the relative commodity-price ratio, a shift of production towards the commodity whose relative price has increased, a rise in the relative price and real income of the factor used intensively in producing that commodity, and a fall in the relative price and real income of the other factor. Thus if a factor-owner group's preferences shift towards the commodity that uses its factor intensively the group's real income and relative income share rises. This point suggests the possibility of

34

collusive action by a factor-owning group to alter its revealed preferences so as to increase its real income by discriminating against consumption of the product that uses its factor unintensively. Concrete examples are 'buy-British' and similar campaigns of discrimination against foreign goods, and union campaigns to induce their members to buy only union-made goods. Where the shift of preferences is exogenous, however, as I have assumed it to be, a distinction must be drawn between changes in the real incomes of factor-owner groups and changes in their economic welfare. A shift of preferences involves a change from one preference system to another, and nothing can be said about welfare in the new equilibrium as compared with welfare in the old unless the indifference curves prevailing in the two situations can be indexed in terms of some underlying quantity of welfare. However, if the preference system of only one factor-owner group changes, the change in the welfare of the other can be identified with the change in its real income.

To turn to the effects of factor accumulation, the main question that arises is whether the conclusion from the one-sector Hicksian model, that an increase in the quantity of a factor must lower its price and raise that of the other factor, continues to hold when the economy produces more than one commodity and can substitute among them. The answer is that it does. This answer rests on two propositions concerning the effects of an increase in the available quantity of a factor, if commodity prices and therefore factor prices are kept constant. The first is that, in this case, all of the additional income consequent on factor augmentation accrues to the owners of the increment of the factor, and by assumption they will wish to spend it on some of both goods, so that demand for both goods increases. The second is the celebrated Rybczynski Theorem,[1] according to which, if commodity prices and therefore factor prices and there-

[1] T. M. Rybczynski, 'Factor Endowment and Relative Commodity Prices', *Economica*, N.S. Vol. XXII, No. 88 (November 1955), pp. 336–41.

fore optimal factor-utilization ratios in the two industries are kept constant, and the quantity of one factor is augmented, maintenance of full employment of both factors requires that the output of the industry that uses the augmented factor intensively must increase in value by more than total output, and the output of the other industry must fall absolutely. Hence, putting the demand and supply consequences of factor increase together, an increase in the quantity of one factor must produce an excess supply of the commodity that uses that factor intensively, and an excess demand for the other, requiring a fall in the relative price of the commodity, and therefore in the relative price, and the marginal product in terms of both commodities, of the factor whose quantity has been increased.

The Rybczynski Theorem can be explained in literary terms as follows: in order for the increment of the augmented factor to earn the price given by the fixed commodity-price ratio, it must be given the appropriate amount of the other factor to work with; and in order to release the required supply of the other factor, the industry using that factor intensively must contract and the industry using the augmented factor intensively expand, keeping employment of the augmented factor constant at the initial level but disemploying some of the unaugmented factor; the amount of the unaugmented factor thus released is then combined with the increment of the augmented factor in further expansion of the industry that uses the augmented factor intensively.

The Theorem can be proved rigorously by use of either of the geometrical constructions employed previously to analyse the production side of the two-sector model. Figure 9 employs the Lerner-Pearce diagram of Figure 3, with the initial endowment of OL_0 of labour and OC_0 of capital, represented by point E, production of X is measured by OP_x and of Y by OP_y. An increase of capital by C_0C_0' shifts the endowment point to E', production of X from P_x to P_x', and production of Y from P_y to

36

P_y'. Figure 10 employs the Edgeworth-Bowley box diagram of Figure 5; at Q, the initial equilibrium production point on the contract curve, the capital-labour ratio in X is the slope of O_xR_x and in Y is the slope of O_yR_y. If capital increases by O_xO_x', and commodity and factor prices and therefore optimal factor-intensities are kept constant, the corresponding point on the new contract curve must lie at the intersection with O_yR_y of

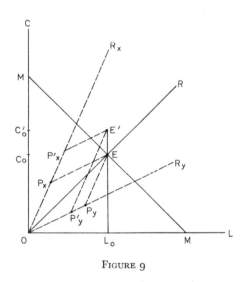

FIGURE 9

$O_x'R_x'$ (which is the vector O_xR_x drawn through the new origin box-corner O_x'), at the point Q'. This point necessarily involves a reduction in the production of Y and an increase in the production of X by more than the value of the total increase in national output.

For completeness, the demand and supply sides of the analysis are put together in Figure 11, which is a version of Figure 8. P_0,C_0 is the initial production and consumption equilibrium of

37

the economy, consistent with income for capital M_cM_c and corresponding consumption point C_c, and income for labour M_LM_L and corresponding consumption point C_L (the derivation of the factor budget lines is not shown, to keep the diagram simple), these consumption points summing by vector addition to total consumption C_0 equal to total production P_0. With an

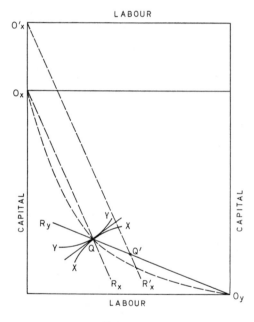

FIGURE 10

increase of capital, prices being kept constant, capital's budget line shifts to $M_c'M_c'$, equal to the increase in the value of output from MM to $M'M'$, capital's consumption point shifts from C_c to C_c', and total consumption demand from C_0 to C_0'. (It is assumed that capital's marginal propensities to consume goods equal its average propensities to consume them, but this is not necessary; any shift to the north-east is consistent with the assumed non-inferiority of goods and produces the same results.) By the Rybczynski Theorem, the production point must shift south-east from P_0 to P_0', along a straight-line locus RR. This locus is the 'Rybczynski line' for increases in capital, and will play an important part in the next lecture. For present purposes, note

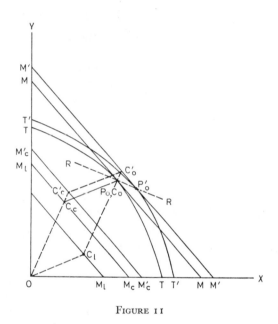

FIGURE 11

only that the north-east shift of C_0 and south-east shift of P_0 entail an excess demand for Y and excess supply of X, requiring a rise in the price of Y and of labour and a fall in the price of X and of capital to restore equilibrium.

Thus, as capital increases, its price must fall and that of labour rise, so that the absolute share of labour must rise. What happens

39

to relative shares, and whether a fall in capital's relative share will go far enough to entail a fall in its absolute share, obviously depends on a far more complex set of parameters than the aggregate elasticity of substitution that determines the movement of relative shares in the one-sector model. But these are not amenable to simple geometrical methods of analysis.

I turn now to technical progress, which for simplicity I shall deal with only in terms of the Lerner-Pearce diagram (which is far the more convenient for the purpose) and which I shall specify in terms of technical progress in the X (capital-intensive) industry. This still leaves three cases for analysis: neutral, capital-saving and labour-saving technical progress. Further, whereas in the case of preference shifts or factor augmentation holding commodity prices constant entailed holding factor prices constant, in the case of technical progress there is a choice between holding commodity prices constant and letting factor prices adjust or holding factor prices constant and letting commodity prices adjust. The latter is the simpler assumption to make, since it entails the commodity price falling in proportion to the degree of technical progress (measured by the cost reduction at the initial factor prices), and I shall employ it for the most part, though I shall indicate some of the possibilities that appear more clearly on the other assumption.

Consider first the case of neutral technical progress in the X industry. Its effect is to shift the X isoquant uniformly proportionately towards the origin, leaving the optimal factor-utilization ratio unchanged if factor prices remain unchanged. Hence the allocation of factors among the industries must remain unchanged, and output of Y remain constant while output of X rises proportionately to the technical progress, if factor prices are to remain unchanged. This is illustrated on Figure 12, where the X-isoquant shifts from XX to $X'X'$, the cost of production of X per unit falls from OM to OM_x, factor utilization ratios remain unchanged at OR_x and OR_y, and hence factor allocations to the two industries (with the given endowment E) remain unchanged at P_x and P_y respectively.

The situation of unchanged factor prices can be an equilibrium position after technical progress only if demand for Y is constant while demand for X expands proportionally to the increase in output. This requires a unitary elasticity of demand for X, elasticity being defined in the Hicksian sense to include both an income and a substitution effect. If the elasticity of

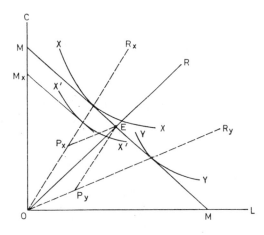

FIGURE 12

demand for X exceeds unity, there will be excess demand for X and supply of Y, the relative price of X and therefore of capital must rise, and therefore the relative and absolute share of capital must rise and that of labour fall, absolute shares being measured in terms of Y, the numéraire. Conversely, if the (Hicksian) elasticity of demand for X is less than unity, the relative price of X must fall, and with it the relative and absolute share of capital, while labour's share increases. It is necessary, however, to distinguish once again between real income and welfare, because the initial reduction in the price of X relative to Y due to technical progress makes the owners of each factor better off, to the extent that they consume X. Consequently, even though a factor's absolute share falls in terms of Y, the economic welfare of its owners may still have increased.

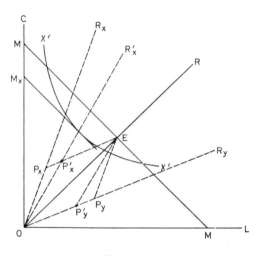

FIGURE 13

Figure 13 depicts the case of capital-saving technical progress, in the X (capital-intensive) industry, i.e. progress which at constant factor prices reduces the ratio of capital to labour employed while reducing the cost of production. Such a reduction, as the figure shows, requires a redeployment of labour and capital from the Y industry into the X industry (the factor allocation points move from P_x to P_x' and from P_y to P_y'); Y production must fall, and X production increase by more than in proportion to the cost-saving brought about by the technical progress. Hence the critical value of the (Hicksian) elasticity of demand for *X*, which determines the movement of relative shares and of absolute shares in terms of the numéraire *Y*, must be something greater than unity.

The opposite holds true for labour-saving innovation in the capital-intensive industry, which is depicted in Figure 14. Here the rise in the capital-labour ratio associated with innovation

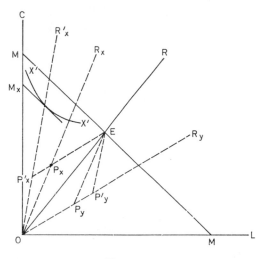

FIGURE 14

requires a redeployment out of the *X* industry into the *Y* industry (shown by the movement from P_x to P_x' and from P_y to P_y'); the output of the *Y* industry must rise, while that of the *X* industry may fall or rise, depending on whether the resource exodus is or is not great enough to offset the improvement in productivity due to the innovation. In any case, the critical value of the Hicksian elasticity of demand for *X* which determines the movement of relative shares and of absolute shares in terms of the numéraire is something less than unity.

43

To summarize the results so far, the effect of technical progress in an industry will be to increase or decrease the relative
share, and the absolute share in terms of the product of the
other industry, of the factor used intensively in that industry,
according as the Hicksian elasticity of demand for the product of
the innovating industry is greater or less than a certain critical
value. That crtitical value will be unity if the innovation is
neutral, greater than unity if the innovation saves the factor

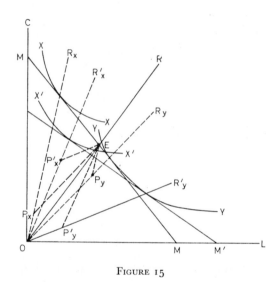

FIGURE 15

used relatively intensively in the industry, and less than unity if
the innovation saves the factor used relatively intensively in the
other industry (i.e. unintensively in the innovating industry).

In the case where the elasticity of demand for the product of
the innovating industry exceeds the critical value, so that the
prices of the product and of the intensively used factor tend to
rise, there is a possibility that the equilibrium product price

44

exceeds that prevailing before the innovation. This possibility can best be investigated on the alternative approach of assuming that the commodity price ratio rather than the factor price ratio is initially fixed. This case is illustrated in Figure 15, which depicts a neutral technical change in the X industry. To keep commodity prices constant, the factor-price ratio must shift from the slope of the common tangent to the pre-innovation isoquants, MM, to that of the common tangent to the new X and old Y isoquants, $M'M'$. This in turn requires changes in the optimal factor-utilization ratios from OR_x and OR_y to OR_x' and OR_y' respectively, and these necessitate a reallocation of resources from the Y industry to the X industry indicated by the movements from P_y to P_y' and P to P_x' respectively. The output of Y falls with the resource shift, while that of X rises for this reason and because of the innovation.

An increase in the output of one industry and reduction of output of the other at constant prices and with rising total income would normally entail an excess supply of the former and demand for the latter, requiring a fall in the relative price of the former to restore equilibrium. But the change in relative factor prices required to maintain constant commodity prices involves a redistribution of income from labour to capital, with capital obtaining more than the whole increase in national income permitted by the innovation; and if capital had a strong marginal preference for X (the capital-intensive good) it would seem that this redistribution effect might increase the demand for X and reduce the demand for Y by more than the associated production changes described. Though I may be wrong, there seems to be nothing in the assumption of stability of equilibrium to exclude this possibility. As the preceding analysis suggests, it is more likely in the case of a labour-saving invention in the capital-intensive X industry than with a neutral invention, and more likely with a neutral invention than with a capital-saving invention in that industry. In more general terms, there is a possibility that an innovation in an industry may raise the equilibrium price of the product of that industry, if the factor used intensively in the industry has a strong relative preference for that product, by comparison with the other factor.

The results of the foregoing analysis of technical progress can be put in another, potentially illuminating way. There is some tendency, at least in popular argument, to assume that technical progress is good or bad for labour, depending on whether it occurs in capital-intensive or labour-intensive industries, or on whether it is biased in the capital-saving or labour-saving direction. The analysis shows that there is no simple way of determining the distribution effects of innovation by its industrial location or factor-saving bias, and that reference must be made in addition to the characteristics of demands for products to answer this kind of question.

Before leaving this aspect of the subject, it is worth noting that if technical progress is assumed for simplicity to be neutrally factor-saving, and to proceed at the same pace in both sectors of the economy, production of both goods will grow at the same rate at constant relative commodity and factor prices, with distributional shares remaining constant and factor real incomes rising at the rate of technical progress. For this to be an equilibrium situation, however, demand for each product must grow proportionately; if the income-elasticity of demand for one of the products is less than unity, the relative price of that product, and of the factor used intensively in producing it, must fall steadily over time. This model, applied to the relation between agriculture and industry in the economy, fits the facts of experience better than the Ricardian assumption of constant technology in agriculture and consequently of an upward trend of rents in response to capital accumulation and population growth.

I turn now from applications of the model to standard problems of distribution theory, involving the effects on distribution of exogenous changes in the data, to applications to the analysis

46

of policies and institutions designed to alter the distribution of income from what would result under perfectly competitive conditions without intervention of any kind.

Consider first the policy of using the government's taxation and spending powers to redistribute income from owners of capital to owners of labour. So long as the tax subsidy policy is general, applying equally to all units of each factor, it does not matter whether the tax takes the form of a proportional sales tax, with proceeds being distributed to labour, or a tax on the earnings of capital, with proceeds being redistributed to labour either directly or as a subsidy on the use of labour. In the former case commodity prices rise relative to factor prices, in the latter case factor prices adjust to absorb the tax or subsidy – though to say this may be misleading, since it implies some sort of monetary numéraire, whereas in a real model there is simply an income transfer from the tax-paying to the subsidized factor. The effect of the income transfer between factors is a standard problem in international trade theory, with the standard answer that production and the factor-price ratio will shift towards that commodity, and the factor it uses intensively, for which the transfer-receiving group has a marginal preference by comparison with the transfer-paying group. The income-redistribution effect of the transfer will therefore be either augmented or mitigated by a factor-price-change effect, depending on whether the labour-owning recipients have a marginal preference for the labour-intensive or the capital-intensive good. The modification of the initial transfer by an adverse factor-price effect cannot, however, fully wipe out the benefit from the transfer, so long as the initial equilibrium is stable.

The analysis is illustrated in Figure 16, based on Figure 8, in which the initial equilibrium of the economy is at P_0C_0, with MM the budget line for the total economy; M_cM_c and M_LM_L are the budget lines of the two groups of factor owners, and

47

C_c and C_L are their equilibrium consumption points, which sum by vector addition to C_0. When $M_cM_c' = M_LM_L'$ of income is redistributed from capital to labour by taxation and subsidy the factor-owners' consumption points shift to C_c' and C_L' respectively (it is assumed for simplicity that the average and marginal

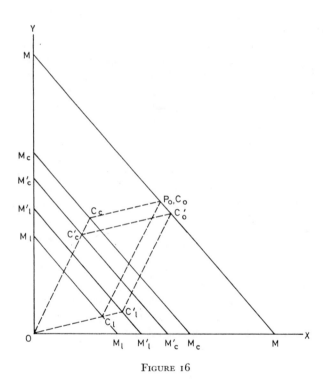

FIGURE 16

propensities to consume of the factor owners are equal). With the redistribution policy, the new community consumption demand point is at C_0', which involves an excess demand for X and supply of Y. To restore general equilibrium, the relative

48

price of X, and with it the relative price of capital, must rise, thereby undoing part of the policy-effected transfer of income from capital to labour. The transfer would instead be increased if the slope of $C_c' C_c$ were less than that of $C_L C_L$, as would be the case if relative marginal propensities to consume were inversely correlated with relative average propensities.

The foregoing analysis assumes that the quantities of the factors available are fixed. If, as might seem reasonable to assume, the quantity of labour supplied falls as a consequence of the receipt of transfer income, this effect by itself will reduce the output of labour-intensive goods and increase that of capital-intensive goods (though not to the same value, owing to the reduction in total labour supplied), thereby tending to create an excess demand for labour and augment the transfer. The two effects of the transfer, in changing the demand and the production pattern, will of course work together if each factor-owner group prefers the commodity that uses it intensively in production, and against each other if the converse assumption holds.

More interesting problems arise, from a theoretical point of view, if the income-redistribution policy is financed, not by a general tax on consumption or on the income on capital, but by a tax on consumption of one commodity only, or a tax on the income of capital in one industry only. In the former case, the tax will shift demand away from the taxed commodity, unless labour has a sufficiently higher marginal propensity to consume the taxed commodity than does capital, to offset the substitution effect tending to reduce both groups' consumption of that good; and if so, labour will derive a secondary benefit from the tax if the taxed good is capital-intensive and a secondary loss if the taxed good is labour-intensive. In the latter event, labour may lose on balance. Where the transfer is financed by a tax on the use of capital in one industry, labour will tend to lose if the tax is imposed on the labour-intensive industry, and gain if it is imposed on the capital-intensive industry, because of the resulting shift of demand between the industries. These remarks are not definitive, however, since the problem really requires explicit mathematical analysis to arrive at a fully satisfactory solution.

Such analysis has not to my knowledge yet been undertaken.[1] Some indication of the complexities and possibilities involved can, however, be gained from analysis of the effects on income distribution of two policies, if I may call them that, that are generally assumed to be effective in redistributing income towards labour; unionization of the labour force, and the imposition of minimum wage laws. These policies derive their theoretical interest from the fact that they are typically applied only to one part of the economy; if both were concerned with raising the real wages of labour above the competitive level, and they applied uniformly across the economy, while capital was fixed in total quantity and distributed itself competitively among industries, the result would necessarily be unemployment of a part of the labour force. Because of their partial application, each can be analysed by use of the two-sector model, on the assumption that the two sectors are now not industries defined in terms of products, but aggregates of industries representing the unionized and non-unionized sectors or subject to and excluded from the minimum wage laws.

[1] The very extensive analysis of the welfare costs and effects of various kinds of taxes by A. C. Harberger, Peter Mieszkowski and others has been conducted on the assumption that such taxes are employed directly by the government and not used for income redistribution. The same is true of an early effort of mine in the general equilibrium analysis of excise taxes, reprinted as Appendix B to this book. Public finance specialists have recently become interested in still another conceptualization of the economics of taxation and public expenditure, which envisages the government as an agency for the collective provision of 'public goods'. The apparatus of the two-sector model of general equilibrium developed in these lectures is applied to the public goods problem in Appendix C.

For the purposes of analysis of the effects of unionization,[1] it is assumed, contrary to the analysis thus far, that the preferences of the various sectors of the community – specifically the owners of capital, of unionized labour, and of non-unionized labour – can be treated as an aggregate community preference system, i.e. that demand effects of income redistributions consequential on unionization can be ignored. This community preference system is further assumed to have two plausible characteristics; that a reduction of real income reduces the quantities of both goods demanded, and that a reduction in the relative price of one commodity causes substitution of that commodity for the other in consumption. Unionization itself is assumed to consist in the introduction of a fixed proportional differential excess of wages in the unionized sector over wages in the non-unionized sector, the number of unionized workers adjusting to demand given this differential. The problem is the effect of unionization so defined on the prices of capital, unionized labour, and non-unionized labour in terms of the products. As will be developed below, analysis of these effects does not constitute a full analysis of the effects of unionization on the distribution of real income.

In the absence of unionization, the production possibilities open to the economy can be depicted by the Edgeworth-Bowley production contract box technique depicted in Figure 5, and reproduced in Figures 17 and 18, in which $O_x P O_y$ is the contract curve in the absence of unionization, and P is assumed to be the general equilibrium production point in those circumstances.

The effect of unionization is to make the wage rate (value of marginal product) in the unionized industry exceed that in the non-unionized industry by a certain proportion. The values of the marginal products of capital in the two industries must,

[1] The analysis here draws on H. G. Johnson and P. Mieszkowski, 'The Effects of Unionization on the Distribution of Income: A General Equilibrium Approach', *The Quarterly Journal of Economics*, Vol. XXXIV, No. 4 (November 1970), pp. 539–61.

however, be equal. In diagrammatic terms, at any point of equilibrium in the allocation of factors between the industries, the slope of the tangent to the isoquant for the unionized industry must be steeper than the slope of the tangent to the isoquant for the non-unionized industry (the slopes being taken with reference to the horizontal, so that they represent the price

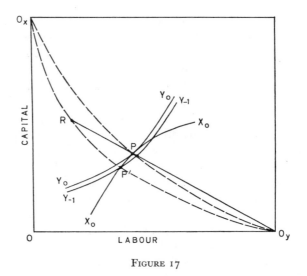

FIGURE 17

of labour in terms of capital). Figures 17 and 18 show such equilibrium points for unionization in the X and Y industries respectively, the points P' in the two figures in each case corresponding to unchanged output in the unionized industry. It is obvious that, because of the differential introduced between the marginal value products of labour in the two industries, the efficiency of production is reduced, and less output of the non-unionized industry is produced for any given output of the unionized industry. In other words, the transformation curve

52

(as derived by the analysis previously presented) is pulled in towards the origin except at its extreme points; it may even become convex to the origin over all or part of its length.[1] Moreover, on the new transformation curve, because of the differential in marginal value products of labour in the two industries introduced by unionization, the private marginal cost of the unionized product exceeds its social marginal cost.

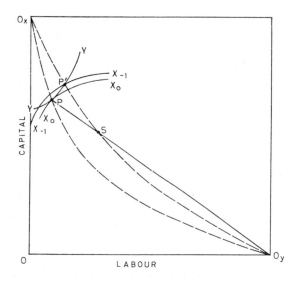

FIGURE 18

Hence the new equilibrium will be doubly inefficient: production will be less than it could be, and consumers will choose inefficiently among points on the transformation curve.

The points P (the pre-unionization general equilibrium

[1] See H. G. Johnson, 'Factor Market Distortions and the Shape of the Transformation Curve', *Econometrica*, Vol. 34, No. 3 (July 1966), pp. 686–98.

production point) and P' (post-unionization equilibrium with production of the pre-unionization quantity of the unionized good) serve as convenient reference points for analysis of the effects of unionization. At P', the capital-labour ratio has risen in the unionized industry and fallen in the non-unionized industry, in comparison with non-unionization. Hence the marginal product of unionized labour in terms of the unionized product must have risen, and the marginal product of non-unionized labour in terms of the non-unionized product must have fallen. The marginal product of capital, correspondingly, must have fallen in terms of the unionized product and risen in terms of the non-unionized product. Since the price of the unionized product must have risen in terms of the non-unionized product, it follows that at point P' as compared with P unionized labour must be receiving wages with an increased purchasing power in terms of both goods, and non-unionized labour wages with a lower purchasing power in terms of both goods. The earnings of capital – which must be the same in value terms in both sectors – are lower in terms of the unionized good and higher in terms of the non-unionized good. Thus, if production were to be maintained at P', unionized labour would be definitely better off, and non-unionized labour definitely worse off, while the owners of capital might be better or worse off depending on the relative quantities in which they consumed the two goods.

By assumption, however, the production point cannot remain at P' (unchanged production of the unionized product) because at that point the community's real income is less than before, owing to the loss of productive efficiency caused by the union distortion of the labour market, while the relative price of the unionized product relative to the non-unionized has risen because of the union wage differential. Production must shift towards less production of the unionized and more production of the non-unionized commodity, with a corresponding re-

54

allocation of factors. The effects of this depend crucially on whether the unionized sector is relatively capital-intensive or relatively labour-intensive. These two alternatives are represented in Figures 17 and 18 respectively.

If the unionized sector is capital-intensive (Figure 17), production shifts along the new contract curve from P' towards O_x. As it does so, the ratio of capital to labour in both industries must rise, so that the marginal products of unionized and non-unionized labour in terms of their own products must rise, while the marginal product of capital in both sectors must fall. That is, by comparison with P', the gains of unionized labour must increase, and the losses of non-unionized labour fall, while capital must become worse off. It is even possible that both groups of labour gain, capital bearing the burden of this loss plus the deadweight loss in the economy's efficiency.

The point R, at which the capital-output ratio is the same as at P, is the dividing line between two sets of possibilities. In the contract curve range $P'R$, the marginal product of capital is higher and of non-union labour lower in the non-unionized product than at P, so that non-union labour is necessarily worse off and capital may be better off than at P. In the range RO_x, the converse holds – the marginal product of capital in the non-unionized product is lower, and of non-unionized labour higher, than at P, so that capital must be worse off and non-union labour may be better off than in the absence of unionization. Where the new equilibrium actually falls will depend on the demand conditions, which I have not specified.

If the unionized sector is labour-intensive (Figure 18), production shifts from P' towards O_y, and the capital-labour ratio falls in both sectors, thus reducing the marginal products of both types of labour in their own sectors and raising the marginal product of capital in both sectors. As a result non-unionized labour must lose by comparison with P', and so must unionized labour; and unionized labour may even lose by comparison with non-unionization, whereas capital may gain unambiguously. The point S divides the new contract curve into two ranges, according to whether the capital-labour ratio in the unionized sector is greater or less than at P. In the range $P'S$, the marginal product of capital in terms of the unionized product is less than at P, so that capital may be worse off. In the range SO_y, the marginal product of capital is higher in both products, so that capital must be better off, while the marginal product of unionized labour in terms of the unionized product is lower than previously, so that unionized labour may itself be made worse off. Where the equilibrium point falls depends as before on the unspecified demand conditions.

In summary, there are two possibilities, depending on whether the union sector is relatively capital-intensive or relatively labour-intensive: unionized labour necessarily better off, and non-unionized labour possibly better off; and non-unionized labour necessarily worse off, and unionized labour possibly worse off. Interestingly enough, in an empirical study of the United States based on the two-sector model, Peter Mieszkowski and I have found the unionized sector to be relatively labour-intensive, and the empirical values of the parameters needed in a quantitative analysis such as to make it possible that unionization has not only harmed the welfare of the non-unionized but reduced the welfare of the unionized as well.[1]

A parallel analysis of the effects of imposing a minimum wage law on a subset of industries reveals a similarly paradoxical result: that, contrary to standard analysis, workers in the industries excluded from the coverage of the law may benefit from it if the industries covered are capital-intensive and if demand conditions have the appropriate configuration.[2]

[1] Johnson and Mieszkowski, *op. cit.*

[2] The analysis draws on H. G. Johnson, 'Minimum Wage Laws: A General Equilibrium Analysis', *The Canadian Journal of Economics*, Vol. II, No. 4 (November 1969), pp. 599–604.

For the purpose of this analysis the same demand assumption is made – that quantity demanded falls with a reduction in real income or a rise in price – and it is assumed that the minimum wage is fixed in terms, not of money, but of the product of the industrial sector covered by the minimum wage. The analysis is illustrated, for the two alternatives of capital-intensity and labour-intensity of the minimum wage sector, by Figures 19 and

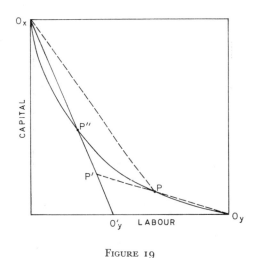

FIGURE 19

20. In each figure, P is the equilibrium production point before the minimum wage law is imposed, and P'' is the position on the pre-law contract curve, corresponding to the minimum wage. In each case the effect of the law is to alter the contract curve to one consisting of two segments: the section of the old curve (O_xP'') for which the marginal product of labour exceeds the minimum wage, and a straight-line section given by the capital-labour ratio in the minimum wage sector required to make labour's marginal product equal to the minimum wage (respec-

57

tively $P''P'O_y'$ and $P''P'O_y$). In neither case can production equilibrium occur in the range O_xP'', because this involves both a lower price and a smaller output of X; it must lie somewhere in the straight-line segment. These segments, however, differ in the price behaviour associated with increased production of X along them. With the minimum wage in X (Figure 19), the price of X must rise as production expands, because the price of

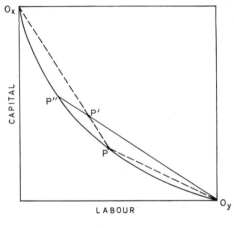

FIGURE 20

labour in the Y industry falls owing to decreasing capital intensity; with the minimum wage in Y (Figure 20), the price of X must fall as production expands, because the price of labour there must fall to absorb excess labour released from the Y industry. Moreover, the relative price of X must be higher at P' than at P in the first case, and lower at P' than at P in the second, because the minimum wage law prevents one of the industries from substituting for capital with the cheaper labour used in the other.

This difference means that in Figure 19 the new production equilibrium may be anywhere beyond P'' on O_xP'' extended, since P' involves both less production of X and a higher price for it than at P, and so could be an equilibrium with a sufficiently elastic demand for X; whereas in Figure 20 equilibrium cannot lie in the segment $P''P'$, since the latter involves both less production and a lower price of X than point P. If the equilibrium lies in the segment $P''P'$ in Figure 19, the capital-labour ratio in the excluded Y sector is higher than at P, so that excluded labour's marginal product in terms of Y is higher than in the absence of the minimum wage in X, and hence this labour may have gained in welfare. This is the exception to the standard conclusion. In Figure 20, the new equilibrium position must lie in the range $O_y P'$, with a lower capital-output ratio and marginal product of labour in the excluded sector than prevailed in the absence of the minimum wage law; and since the relative price of the product of that sector must also be lower than under competitive equilibrium, labour in the excluded sector is made unambiguously worse off by the minimum wage law.

The traditional conclusion that an effective minimum wage law applied throughout the economy must produce unemployment can be demonstrated easily by drawing a second vector from the relevant origin through P''. P'' cannot represent an equilibrium position, since it involves both a lower output and a lower price of X than the point P. But with fixed coefficients in both industries, the only way to increase production of X and decrease production of Y is to shift the origin O_x closer to the right so that the ray $O_x P''$ intersects the ray $O_y P''$ closer to the Y origin – and this entails unemployment of labour.

In this lecture I have applied the two-sector model of production and distribution developed in my first lecture to some standard problems of distribution theory and to the effects of policies and institutions designed to alter the distribution of income. In my third lecture I shall convert the model into a growth model, and use it to explore some of the problems of growth theory.

III

A Two-Sector Model of Economic Growth

In my first two lectures, I have developed the two-sector model of production and distribution and applied it to the analysis both of standard problems in the theory of distribution – changes in tastes, factor supplies, and technology – and of various policies designed to influence the distribution of income among the owners of the two factors of production. The analysis has been, technically, a comparative statics analysis, in the sense that factor supplies and technology have been taken as exogenously given, or subject to exogenously given change. For this lecture, I shall open the model out into a dynamic model of economic growth, though to a limited extent only, by assuming that the stock of capital available to the economy is determined by the savings behaviour of the community. I shall not make the model fully dynamic, however, because I shall follow the tradition of at least the simpler of contemporary growth models by assuming, first, that the rate of population growth is exogenously given, and second, that the rate of technical progress is not only exogenously given but takes a particular form – convenient for theory but not necessarily realistic – namely the form of purely labour-augmenting or 'Harrod-neutral' technical progress. These assumptions I shall, however, relax at particular points in the argument to indicate how the analysis can be applied to some problems of growth in the contemporary world.

Before I open the model up in this way, however, I should like to spend a little time on the one-sector models I discussed in my first lecture.

The Ricardian model is, of course, the quintessential growth model, and the basis of classical and neo-classical theorizing about growth, even though it is formulated in comparative statics terms. In that model, in contrast to contemporary growth models, population growth is a dependent rather than an independent variable, and technology is a given constant rather than an exogenous variable; of these two differences, the former rather than the latter constitutes a significant difference from contemporary growth models, because a zero rate of technological progress is only a particular case of an exogenously given rate of technical progress. With population a dependent variable, growth can be limited only by some exogenous influence that depresses the rate of return on capital and consequently brings the propensity to accumulate to a halt. In the Ricardian system, this influence is the fixed quantity of land in conjunction with the fixity of technology, which implies diminishing marginal productivity of labour applied to land, and, given the perfect elasticity of supply of labour, a diminishing rate of return on the wages fund as that fund accumulates. By contrast, with the rate of population growth exogenously given (and the rate of labour-augmenting technical progress also), it is no longer necessary to make the assumption (which in contemporary industrial society appears unrealistic) that the land factor is fixed in quantity. Instead, the falling rate of profit is deduced from the operation of diminishing returns as capital accumulates relative to the 'effective labour force' (which, in turn, grows at the sum of the rates of natural population increase, and of Harrod-neutral technical progress, appropriately defined).

The Hicksian model of distribution, as already mentioned,

is a comparative-statics model of distribution between capital and labour on the assumption of a constant-returns to scale technology. It can, however, readily be converted into a growth model by assuming, first, that either the working population grows at an exogenously given natural rate of increase, technology being given, or that the 'effective' working population grows at a rate given exogenously by the sum of the natural rate of population increase and the rate of Harrod-neutral (purely labour-augmenting) technical progress; second, that the single output of the economy can be used either for consumption or for capital investment – in this connection, it simplifies the analysis, without loss of generality, to assume that capital equipment once installed lasts for ever, so that problems of depreciation can be ignored; and third, that the accumulation of capital is governed either by the existence of a fixed ratio of savings to total income (or output), or by the Ricardian mechanism according to which the economy accumulates capital so long as the rate of return on it exceeds a certain minimum rate which we would now regard as being determined by the 'minimum social rate of time preference'. I personally do not find the fixed savings ratio assumption congenial, since on the one hand it is not derived from utility-maximization considerations, and on the other hand the historical evidence for a constant savings ratio is consistent with a number of different theories of saving based on rational utility-maximization. Still, since it is the conventional assumption in the growth-model literature, I shall use it for the main part of the analysis of the one-sector model, referring only briefly to the alternative Ricardian assumption that savings behaviour is governed by a minimum rate of time preference.[1]

[1] For a fuller analysis of the model to be presented, including the introduction of money, see Harry G. Johnson 'Money in a Neo-Classical Growth Model', Chapter IV, pp. 143–78 in *Essays in Monetary Economics* (London: Allen & Unwin, 1967).

The one-sector model of economic growth is depicted in Figure 21, where Oy represents output per head of the effective labour force (assumed to increase at an exponential rate n as a result of the combined effects of population growth and Harrod-neutral technical progress) and $O.sy$ represents saving per head at different levels of output per head, determined by the fixed savings ratio s. The ray $O.nk$ represents what may be

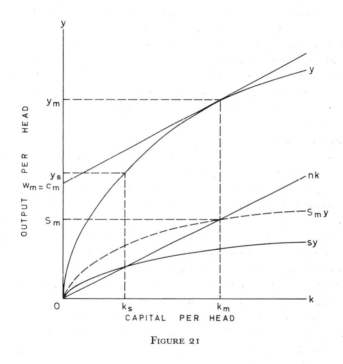

FIGURE 21

termed the capital or investment requirement of constant output per head: a proportion n of the existing stock of capital per head must be invested if capital per head (and therefore output per head) is to remain constant as the effective labour force grows over time.

Given the savings ratio, the economy will converge on a long-run equilibrium position (in per capita terms) determined by the intersection of the savings curve and the capital requirements curve, with capital per head of the effective labour force k_s and output per head of the effective labour force y_s. The necessity of convergence on this equilibrium can be seen by considering any arbitrary initial level of capital per head. If the initial level is to the left of k_s, savings per head exceeds the investment required to keep capital per (effective) head constant, and the level of capital per head must grow over time; conversely, if the initial level of capital per head is to the right of k_s, the investment requirement exceeds saving per head and capital per head must shrink over time; the increase or decrease of capital per head will cease when savings per head become equal to the investment requirement.

Since the economy must converge on an equilibrium level of capital and output per (effective) head of population, with the aggregate growth rate determined by the rate of growth of the effective labour force, determined exogenously by the rates of natural increase and Harrod-neutral technical progress, the growth rate ceases to be of theoretical interest. This, incidentally, is an important point for economic policy. Much theory and policy-making in the past two decades has been devoted to methods of increasing the rate of economic growth; but the model demonstrates that policy-induced increases in the growth rate can only be transitional, unless policy is aimed either at increasing the rate of population growth – which virtually no one would regard as desirable – or at increasing the rate of technical progress – which is a more complex problem than altering savings and investment behaviour, which is the usual focus of growth-oriented economic policy.

In place of the growth rate, which is in the long run exo-

64

genously determined, economic interest centres on the characteristics of the steady-state growth path of the economy, and specifically on the level of consumption per head enjoyed in the course of long-run equilibrium growth. By assumption, as capital per head grows, so does output per head; but so also does the investment requirement. Moreover, the investment requirement grows proportionally with capital per head, whereas output per head grows less than proportionally with capital per head. The difference between output and the investment requirement is the level of consumption per head that can be maintained in perpetuity; and for the reasons just given it must first grow and then decline as capital per head increases, being subject to a technically determined maximum. (The determining factors are the technology that determines the shape of the relation between capital and output per head, and the exogenously given growth rate that determines the investment requirement.) The interesting theoretical question, therefore, concerns the conditions required for maximum 'permanent' consumption per head. This maximum is determined diagrammatically by parallelism of the tangent to the Oy curve with the investment requirements curve $O.nk$, yielding output per head Oy_m and requiring investment per head OS_m, corresponding to the savings ratio s_m with consumption per head $S_m y_m = Ow_m$. The slope of $O.nk$ is n, the rate of growth; and the slope of the Oy curve is the marginal product of capital, which, because output and capital are measured in the same units, and capital lasts for ever, is the rate of return on capital or the rate of interest. Hence one statement of the condition for maximization of consumption per head is that accumulation should be carried to the point where the rate of interest equals the (exogenously given) rate of growth of the economy. Another statement of the condition follows from the observation that $y_m w_m$ is the absolute share of capital per man in the total product per man (its marginal product multiplied by its quantity per man) and

E   65

Ow_m the absolute share of labour per man; from this it follows that maximum consumption per head will be achieved if the share of labour is entirely consumed and the share of capital is entirely invested. This result will ensue automatically if, following the Marxist tradition, it is assumed that capitalists reinvest all their profits and workers consume all their wages; but the result could equally well be achieved by proper regulation of the total saving of the economy.

The conditions for maximum permanent consumption per head just developed are described in the literature as the 'golden rule' conditions (alternatively, as the 'neo-neo-classical growth theorem'). But it is important to realize that they are technical conditions, and not normative rules or prescriptions. They have to be interpreted in the following sense. If an economy were to the right of the 'golden rule' capital per head level k_m, it could raise its consumption per head immediately and at all future points of time by reducing its savings ratio to the 'golden rule' ratio S_m; hence in this case the 'golden rule' is a normative prescription for increasing welfare, unless society is assumed to derive utility from the possession of property independently of its consumption goods yield. But if the economy is to the left of the 'golden rule' position, the increase in its savings ratio required to raise it in the long run to that position would entail a sacrifice of immediate consumption for the sake of higher future consumption; and this would involve an intertemporal choice between present and future consumption, the basis for which is not provided by the model. Since most societies can reasonably be assumed to fall short of the golden rule position – rates of return on capital typically exceed growth rates of gross national product – the 'golden rule' conditions provide no guidance to current economic policy.

The foregoing analysis has assumed that society is characterized by a fixed ratio of saving to income. However, to any such savings ratio there corresponds an equilibrium rate of

66

return on capital, and the fixed savings ratio assumption can therefore easily be replaced by the assumption that society accumulates capital until the rate of return is equalized with a minimum social rate of time preference. On this assumption, the 'golden rule' condition is that society's rate of time preference be equal to its exogenously given rate of increase of the effective labour force. To ensure convergence on a steady-state growth path in this model, however, it is necessary to assume that a divergence of the actual rate of return on capital from the minimum rate of time preference results in sufficient saving or dissaving to move the actual rate of return on capital towards the rate of time preference.

Reverting to the fixed savings ratio assumption, it might seem potentially more interesting to assume that different savings ratios apply to the incomes of capital and labour (that of capital income being higher), since then the characteristics of the production function could be such as to redistribute income towards capital as accumulation proceeds, thereby raising the ratio of savings to income and permitting the savings curve to cut the investment requirement curve from below. This would require an elasticity of substitution greater than unity, and if it happened would imply the possibility of multiple growth equilibria alternatively stable, unstable, and stable. However, this possibility can be ruled out.[1] Hence discussion of the implications of differing savings ratios is deferred until the analysis of the two-sector model where the change in assumption from a single aggregate savings ratio can raise important difficulties.

The one-sector model just presented can be easily adapted to represent two theories of the problem of economic development, according to which the initiation of growth of income per capita requires an initial 'big push' of investment to get the

[1] On this point see Harry G. Johnson 'Money in a Neo-Classical Growth Model', p. 149, n. 1 in *Essays in Monetary Economics* (London: Allen & Unwin, 1967), and the Mathematical Appendix to this book.

economy over a hump and on to a more promising growth path. According to one such theory, limited efforts at development will be frustrated by accelerated population growth, and the economy must be raised to a level of per capita income at which the general population will voluntarily choose family limitation for the sake of material improvement. This theory is illustrated in Figure 22, where the rate of population increase is assumed to be first an increasing function, then a decreasing function, and then independent, of income per capita. An

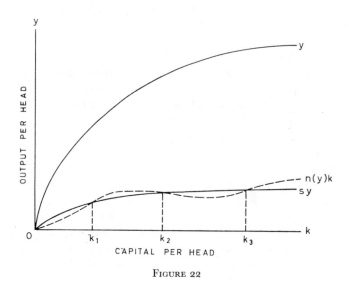

FIGURE 22

alternative theory, illustrated in Figure 23, is that while there are diminishing returns to capital per head in the neighbourhood of low-level equilibrium, a sufficiently large increase in capital per head will bring the economy into a region of increasing returns to scale. In each figure, k_1 represents the initial low-level equilibrium of capital and output per head, k_3 the attainable high-level equilibrium position, and k_2 the intervening 'hump' position of unstable equilibrium which the economy must somehow surmount if it is to put itself on the path towards high-level equilibrium growth.

The one-sector model of economic growth just analysed has the theoretical advantages that the rate of return on capital is a

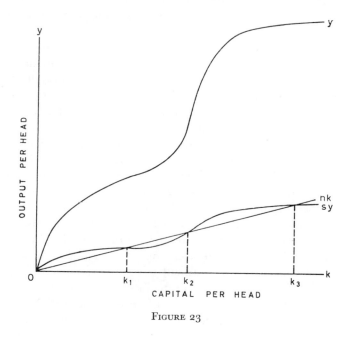

FIGURE 23

unique function of the stock of capital per head, and independent of the rate of current saving and investment, and that a given savings ratio applied to the output from a given stock of capital per head implies a unique rate of production of capital goods. In both cases, the reason is the fixed (unitary) rate of exchange between consumption goods and investment goods implicit in the aggregation of output into a single good. In the two-sector model of growth, to which I now turn, the (instantaneous) rate of return on capital depends on the allocation of production between investment and consumption, and the rate of production of investment goods is not uniquely determined by the savings ratio but depends also on the relative price of investment goods in terms of consumption goods, which in turn has to be determined by a general equilibrium adjustment process. The two-sector model also makes interesting the question of the effects on the growth process of differences in the savings ratios of the two groups of factor owners, capital and labour; this question I shall defer until later, treating saving initially as a matter of aggregate community behaviour.[1]

The two-sector model of general equilibrium developed in the previous lectures can be converted into a growth model by assuming that the effective labour force grows at a constant rate (as a result of natural increase and Harrod-neutral technical progress[2]) and that capital accumulation is determined endogenously by a given savings ratio or minimum rate of time preference. It simplifies matters to assume that capital equipment is, besides being perfectly malleable (to allow for substitution between capital and labour), permanent in duration; permanent durability is not a significant restriction of the analysis, since replacement investment on any reasonable theory of depreciation can be included in the investment required to keep the capital stock per capita intact. As in the case of the other applications of the two-sector model developed in the preceding lecture, it turns out that the alternative possible assumptions

[1] As already mentioned, differences in the savings ratios of the two groups of factor owners have no interesting implications for the behaviour of a one-sector growth model.

[2] Technical progress must be assumed not only to be Harrod-neutral, but to proceed at the same rate in the two industries.

about the relative capital-intensities of the two sectors are crucial to the results.[1]

As with the one-sector model, the process of growth in a two-sector model is most conveniently approached in terms of variations in the stock of capital per head of the effective labour force. For any given stock of capital per head, there will be a

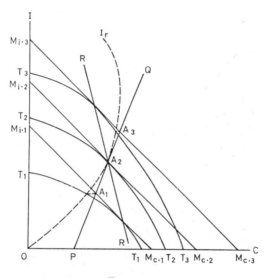

FIGURE 24

per capita transformation curve between investment goods and consumption goods. The transformation curves for successively

[1] The model to be presented has been developed and applied to international trade theory in two earlier articles of mine: 'Trade and Growth: A Geometrical Analysis', in J. Bhagwati, R. W. Jones, R. A. Mundell and J. Vanek (eds.), *Trade, Balance of Payments and Welfare: Essays in Honour of C. P. Kindleberger* (Cambridge: M.I.T. Press 1971); 'Trade and Growth: A Geometrical Exposition', *The Journal of International Economics*, Vol. I, No. 1 (January–March 1971).

larger stocks of capital per head will be outside one another, in such a fashion that, if a given price ratio between investment goods and consumption goods is selected, points on the successive transformation curves with a slope equal to that price ratio will lie along a straight line, the 'Rybczynski line' for that commodity-price ratio and the corresponding factor-price ratio. If the investment good is relatively capital-intensive in

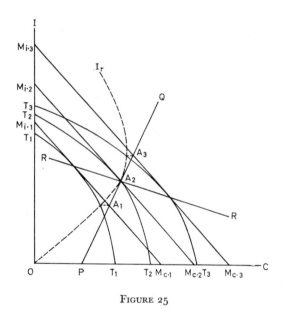

FIGURE 25

production, the Rybczynski line RR will slope upwards to the north-west as shown in Figure 24; if the investment good is relatively labour-intensive in production, the Rybczynski line will slope downwards to the south-east, as shown in Figure 25.

For the arbitrarily chosen price ratio between investment and consumption goods, there will be for each transformation curve a corresponding budget line representing the community's income, the terminal points of which represent the value in terms of the two goods respectively of the income producible with the stock of capital per head that determines the location of the transformation curve. These budget lines are represented in Figures 24 and 25 by $M_{I.1} M_{C.1}$, $M_{I.2} M_{C.2}$, etc. On each such budget line there will be a point representing the quantity of investment goods that must be produced to keep the stock of capital per head constant over time; as in the one-sector model, this quantity will be the existing stock of capital per head multiplied by n, the rate of growth of the effective labour force. These points are represented in the figures by A_1, A_2, A_3. Such points will lie along a straight-line locus PQ, intersecting the horizontal axis to the right of the origin O. The locus is a straight line because, with a given commodity and factor-price ratio (and hence constant marginal product of capital) both income and the investment required to keep capital per head intact increase in proportion to the quantity of capital; it intersects the horizontal axis to the right of O because, again with fixed factor prices, a fixed part of income is attributable to the services of labour. This part is represented by the distance OP; it can be thought of as the output that labour alone would produce if it could hire capital at the rental price corresponding to the arbitrarily chosen commodity and factor-price ratio.

The budget lines $M_I M_C$, and the locus PQ, are constructed on the assumption of an arbitrary price ratio. PQ cannot, in fact, represent the combinations of investment and consumption goods the economy can produce with different stocks of capital, subject to the condition of keeping capital per head intact, because these combinations must lie on the transformation curves corresponding to the different stocks of capital per head. Instead, PQ is merely a reference line, from which the locus of combinations of investment and consumption goods the economy will produce with different capital stocks and keeping capital per head intact is constructed by drawing horizontal lines from the points A_1,

73

A_2, A_3, etc., to the transformation curves tangent to the budget lines on which these points lie. Such horizontal lines trace out the curve $O.A_2.I_r$, which is termed 'the investment requirement curve' and shows the relation between consumption goods production and the investment goods production required to keep capital per head intact as the capital stock per head increases.

As is evident from the construction in the two figures, the investment requirement curve must be concave towards the horizontal axis, and further must eventually bend back on itself as capital per head increases. This latter property is the consequence of the assumption of diminishing returns to increases in the ratio of capital to labour in the two industries. The point at which the investment requirement curve becomes vertical shows the maximum consumption per head that the economy can technically attain – the 'golden rule' position. At this point, the whole of the output of a marginal increment of capital is required to produce the additional investment goods required to keep capital per head intact. The marginal product of capital in producing investment goods is the own rate of return on capital or the rate of interest, while the increment in the capital requirement per unit increment of capital is n, the exogenously-given rate of increase of the effective labour force. Hence we derive the 'golden rule' condition for the maximization of consumption per head along the economy's equilibrium growth path, equality of the rate of interest with the exogenously-given steady-state equilibrium growth rate. Further, by multiplying both sides of the equation by the value of capital (measured in either investment goods or consumption goods) we obtain the alternative form of the condition, that aggregate saving and investment should equal the total income of capital; and by then dividing each side by income (measured in the same units of investment or consumption goods) we obtain a third alternative formulation, that the savings ratio should be equal to the share of capital in total income.

The investment requirement curve shows the long-run-equilibrium consumption-per-head possibilities open to the economy, and the corresponding levels of investment goods production necessary to sustain these possibilities. The levels of capital stock and consumption and investment goods production per head actually attained will depend on the savings behaviour of the community. Initially, we take the savings behaviour to be represented by a fixed aggregate ratio of saving to income.

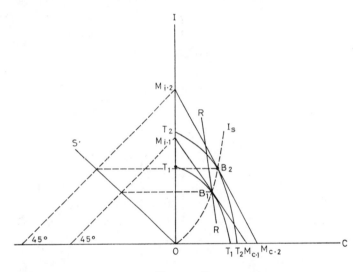

FIGURE 26

In contrast to the one-sector model, in which the value of income per head is uniquely determined by capital per head and the amount of investment per head is uniquely determined by income per head and the savings ratio, in the two-sector model the value of output for a given capital stock per head and the amount of investment are interdependent with the savings

75

ratio. In Figures 26 and 27, the line OS on the left-hand side of the diagram is so drawn that, for any level of income OM_I measured in terms of the investment good, a line with a negative slope of 45° through M_I intersects OS at a point showing the level of saving and investment determined by the fixed saving ratio of the economy. For any transformation curve corresponding to a given stock of capital per head, such as T_1T_1, general equilibrium of the economy requires that the production point

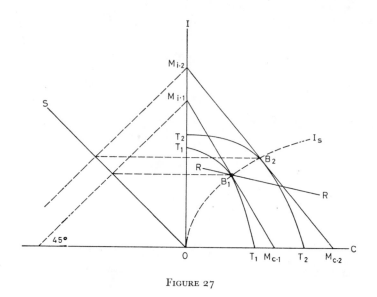

FIGURE 27

B_1 be such that, when output is evaluated at the relative prices prevailing at that point, the resulting income measured in terms of the investment good, $OM_{I,1}$, when multiplied by the fixed savings ratio, results in a quantity of investment goods demanded equal to the output of these goods at the point B_1. The equilibrium quantities of investment goods demanded, as determined by

76

the savings ratio, from the incomes producible with successively larger capital stocks per head trace out what may be termed 'the investment supply curve', OI_s. Every point on the investment supply curve represents a unique stable equilibrium, given the amount of capital per head, because a shift of production towards investment goods would raise the ratio of the value of investment goods production to the value of total output, while leaving the savings ratio unchanged, and vice versa.

If the investment good is capital-intensive as in Figure 26, an increase in income at constant prices would move the consumption and investment demand-equilibrium point of the economy outwards from B_1 along a vector OB, through the origin O, while it would move the consumption and investment production equilibrium point north-west along the Rybczynski line through B_1. To restore equilibrium between production and consumption, the quantity of investment goods produced must fall and demanded must rise by comparison with these positions, implying both a more than proportional increase in income measured in investment goods to $OM_{I.2}$ and a more than proportional increase in the equilibrium quantity of investment goods demanded and supplied to the equilibrium point B_2. Consequently in this case the investment supply curve must be concave towards the vertical axis. Conversely, if the investment good is labour-intensive, as in Figure 27, the investment supply curve must be convex to the vertical axis (concave to the horizontal axis).

The steady-state growth path equilibrium of the economy is determined by the intersection of the investment requirements curve and the investment supply curve, as indicated in Figures 28 and 29 for the two cases of capital-intensity and labour-intensity of the investment goods industry respectively. In the diagrams, TT is the steady-state growth equilibrium tranformation curve per capita, $M_I M_c$ the budget line depicting the value of income, PQ the reference-locus investment requirement curve at the equilibrium price ratio between investment and consumption goods, and *OS* the income-expansion line depicting the division of demand for output between investment goods and consumption goods determined by the commodity-price ratio and the fixed savings ratio of the community.

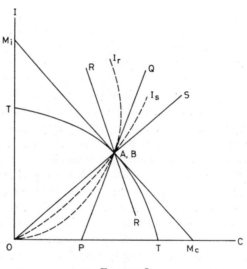

FIGURE 28

In the case of labour-intensive investment goods production, the concavity of the I_s curve to the vertical axis in conjunction with the convexity of the I_r curve to the same axis ensures that the long-run growth equilibrium of the economy is unique. In the case of capital-intensive investment goods production, however, both the I_s and I_r curves are concave to the vertical axis, and it is possible for them to intersect more than once (necessarily an odd number of times), indicating the possibility of multiple steady-state growth equilibria. These equilibria will be alternatively stable and unstable, instability in this context meaning that any departure of the capital stock per head from the equilibrium level will start the economy expanding or contracting its capital per head towards the adjoining stable equilibrium position. The possibility of an unstable equilibrium is evident from Figure 28 from the fact that the investment requirement line must lie between the Rybczynski line and the income-expansion line OS, so that the equilibrium savings-consumption

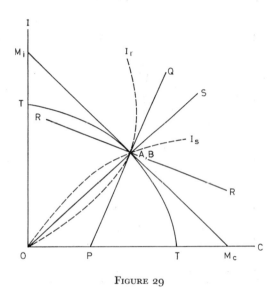

FIGURE 29

position with an expanded capital stock may involve a higher or lower rate of production of investment goods than is required to keep the (augmented) capital stock intact. Presumably, if the process of accumulation proceeds slowly enough, the economy will come into long-run growth equilibrium at the lower capital stock per head and higher interest rate represented by the position of stable equilibrium closest to the origin.

79

The analysis of the two-sector growth model thus far has assumed that the accumulation behaviour of the economy is governed by a constant savings ratio applied to the economy's total income. The alternative interesting assumption is that the economy's savings behaviour is governed by a minimum rate of time preference; for this model to produce the possibility of a steady-state growth equilibrium, it is necessary to assume that an excess of the actual over the minimum rate of time preference

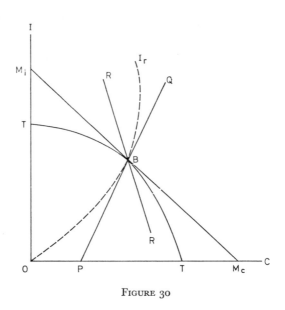

FIGURE 30

produces a rate of current saving sufficient to increase capital per head, and vice versa, while the economy keeps capital per head constant when the rate of return on capital is equal to the minimum rate of time preference.

On this assumption, possible long-run equilibrium points for production per head lie on the Rybczynski line for the commodity and factor-price ratio corresponding to the minimum rate of time preference; and the investment requirements curve can be drawn as the straight-line reference curve for that price ratio. The analysis is illustrated, for the two cases of capital-intensity and labour-intensity of the investment good, in Figures 30 and 31 respectively.

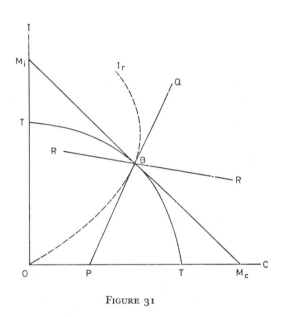

FIGURE 31

In each case, the intersection of the investment requirements line PQ with the savings behaviour line (the relevant Rybczynski line) at the point B indicates the position of long-run steady-state growth equilibrium; this position must be unique. However, only in the case of the investment good being labour-intensive is the long-run equilibrium position stable. In Figure 31, a temporary increase of capital per head

F

beyond the equilibrium level, and hence a movement of the budget line north-east of $M_I M_c$, would produce a reduction of the equilibrium output of investment goods corresponding to the minimum rate of time preference below the corresponding investment requirement. Further, an increase in the rate of production of investment goods would reduce the rate of return on capital below the economy's minimum rate of time preference, thereby evoking disinvestment in capital per head. Thus the temporary divergence from long-run steady-state equilibrium would be corrected by disinvestment (or, in the converse case, accumulation of capital per head).

In Figure 30, however, a temporary increase in capital and income per head entails an increase in output of the investment good above the investment requirement (at constant prices and the time-preference minimum interest rate); and an increase in the rate of investment above the rate required to keep initial capital per head constant entails a rise in the price of investment goods, and therefore the current rate of return on capital, and therefore an accumulation of capital per head of an explosive sort. The converse holds for a temporary decrease in capital and income per head. Hence the case of capital-intensity of the investment good must be ruled out if savings behaviour is to be dealt with in terms of a simple time-preference model. (Of course, stability of equilibrium could probably be restored to the model by a sufficiently careful specification of the process of adjustment of actual to desired capital stock through current saving and investment.)

Up to this point, I have assumed that the economy's accumulation behaviour can be treated in aggregative terms, and expressed either in terms of an aggregate ratio of savings to income or of an aggregate minimum rate of time preference. One of the main interests in distinguishing between factors, and factor-owner groups, in economics however has been to examine the consequences of differences in the accumulative behaviour of these groups – typically, following Ricardo and Marx, the consequences of the assumption that capitalists save and workers do not. On that crude assumption, capitalist accumulation behaviour is the key to understanding of the long-run behaviour of accumulation and distribution in a capitalist economy. If, on the other hand, both groups are assumed to save, but capitalists are assumed more prone to saving than workers, some interesting theoretical possibilities are opened up. This assumption, however, raises some definitional problems, since workers who save become in part at least capitalists themselves, and the difference between the two groups becomes that the capitalists derive income only from their ownership of capital, with no income from labour services. To put the point another way, differences in savings behaviour have to be related to differences between the two kinds of income, rather than to differences between social classes: 'capitalists' become those who dispose of income from capital, and 'workers' those who dispose of income from labour, and the same individual may be both simultaneously.

If each group of income-receivers is assumed to accumulate according to a minimum rate of time preference, and the higher savings proclivities of 'capitalists' are reflected in a lower minimum rate of time preference, it is obvious that 'workers' will hold capital only transitionally, and that in the long run the rate of interest will be reduced to the 'capitalist' minimum rate of time preference, with no savings being made from labour income and no wealth being held by recipients of labour income.

If, instead, the economy is assumed to apply one savings ratio to income from capital, and another (lower) ratio to income from labour, a new problem is introduced, namely that the redistribution of income associated with a movement along a given transformation curve (corresponding to a given stock of capital per head) may operate to increase demand for the product towards which production has shifted, thereby giving rise to

83

the possibility of multiple equilibrium. This is of course merely an example of the general possibility of multiple equilibrium discussed in the first lecture, for the special case in which each factor-owning group divides its expenditure in a fixed proportion between the two commodities in the system.[1]

It should be noted that this is a different problem than the possibility of multiple steady-state growth equilibria, which has already been shown to be excluded by the assumption that investment goods production is labour-intensive, but permitted by the assumption that investment goods production is capital-intensive, in the case of a single aggregate savings ratio. The difficulty it poses is that in the course of accumulative movement towards the steady-state growth path, the economy may have to make a discontinuous 'jump' from one stable-equilibrium accumulative path to another, through an intervening unstable-equilibrium accumulation path, stability here being defined as stability of savings-investment equilibrium with a given stock of capital per head and the paths in question representing the effects on savings-investment behaviour of the accumulation of capital per head. As it turns out, this possibility, like the possibility of multiple steady-state growth equilibria, depends on the investment goods sector being capital-intensive.

If the investment good is labour-intensive, an increase of production of it from an initial equilibrium point (which may be stable or unstable) must increase the ratio of the value of production of it to the total value of output, by raising both its quantity and its relative price. But such an increase must raise the relative price of labour and reduce that of capital, thereby reducing the ratio of aggregate saving to aggregate income. Hence such an equilibrium must be stable, and therefore unique.

If on the other hand the investment good is capital-intensive,

[1] For a fuller discussion see G. H. Borts, 'Professor Meade on Economic Growth', *Economica*, N.S. Vol. 29, No. 113 (February 1962), pp. 72–86.

a shift towards more production of it from an initial equilibrium point (which may be stable or unstable) must equally increase the ratio of the value of production of it to the value of total production; but it must in this case raise the relative price of capital and lower the relative price of labour, thereby re-distributing income towards capital-owners and raising the proportion of aggregate income saved. This increase in the savings ratio may exceed the increase in the investment ratio, thereby indicating that the initial equilibrium is unstable and signalling the presence of multiple equilibria. The question then is the conditions under which the rise in the production of investment goods must exceed the increase in demand for them, guaranteeing stability and hence uniqueness of the initial equilibrium.

The proportion of income saved in the economy can be written as

$$s = (s_K - s_L)\,(Q_{I.K}\,I + Q_{C.K}C) + S_L$$
$$= (s_K - s_L)\,[Q_{I.K} - Q_{C.K})\,I + Q_{C.K}] + S_L$$

where s is the aggregate savings ratio, s_C and s_L are respectively the savings ratios from capital and labour income, I and C are the ratios of the values of output of investment and consumption goods to total output $(I + C = 1)$, and $Q_{I.K}$ and $Q_{C.K}$ are the shares of capital in income from investment goods output and consumption goods output respectively (with $Q_{I.K}$ greater than $Q_{C.K}$ by assumption, and both necessarily less than unity).

It is obvious from the formulae that the share of total savings in income (s) must increase by less than the share of the value of investment goods in the value of output (I) when the price of investment goods and the rate of return on capital rise, so long as the shares of capital in the values of output in the two sectors do not rise when the price of capital rises. The condition necessary to ensure this is that the elasticity of substitution between capital and labour in each sector be greater than unity,

85

so that a factor's relative share falls as its relative price rises; or, more generally, that an appropriately weighted average of the elasticities of substitution in the two sectors be greater than unity.

Thus, in order to exclude the possibility of multiple short-run equilibria (i.e. equilibria with given capital stock per head), it is necessary (sufficient though not necessary in the mathematical sense) to assume either that the investment goods industry is labour-intensive – which has the additional theoretical advantage of ensuring a unique steady-state growth equilibrium – or that the elasticities of substitution between capital and labour in the two production functions are each (or on an appropriately weighted average) greater than unity.

Mathematical Notes on the One-Sector Model

(a) *The Hicksian Model of Distribution*

Let $x = f(a, b)$ be the aggregate production function where x is aggregate output and a and b are the quantities of the two factors.

The aggregate production function is assumed to be linear homogeneous (subject to constant returns to scale). This implies

$$x = af_a + bf_b \tag{1}$$

$$f_{ab} = -\frac{a}{b}f_{aa} = -\frac{b}{a}f_{bb} \tag{2}$$

$$\sigma = \frac{f_a f_b}{x f_{ab}} \tag{3}$$

where subscripts denote differentiation of the production function by the subscripted argument or arguments, and σ is the elasticity of substitution. (For proofs see R. G. D. Allen, *Mathematical Analysis for Economists*, pages 317 and 343.) By the usual assumptions $f_{ab} > 0$, and $f_{aa}, f_{bb} < 0$.

Define $K_a = af_a$, $K_b = bf_b$, the absolute shares of the factors, and $k_a = af_a/x$, $k_b = bf_b/x$, the relative shares of the factors,

$$\frac{dK_a}{da} = f_a + af_{aa}$$

$$= f_a\left(1 - \frac{bf_{ab}}{f_a}\right)$$

$$= f_a\left(1 - \frac{bf_b}{x} \cdot \frac{1}{\sigma}\right)$$

$$= f_a\left(\frac{\sigma - k_b}{\sigma}\right)$$

$$= f_a\left(\frac{k_a - (1 - \sigma)}{\sigma}\right) \tag{4}$$

$$\frac{dK_a}{db} = af_{ab} = \frac{1}{\sigma}\frac{af_af_b}{x} \tag{5}$$

By (5) an increase in the quantity of one factor must always increase the absolute share of the other. By (4) an increase in the quantity of one factor will increase that factor's absolute share unless the elasticity of substitution is smaller than the relative share of the other factor, or (alternatively) unless the elasticity of substitution is below unity by more than the relative share of the augmented factor.

$$\frac{dk_a}{da} = \frac{1}{x}\left(x(f_a + af_{aa}) - af_a(f_a + af_{aa} + bf_{ab})\right)$$

$$= \frac{1}{x^2}\left(bf_b(f_a + af_{aa}) - af_abf_{ab}\right)$$

$$= \frac{b}{x^2}\left(f_af_b - bf_bf_{ab} - af_af_{ab}\right)$$

$$= \frac{b}{x^2}f_af_b\left(1 - \frac{xf_{ab}}{f_af_b}\right)$$

$$= \frac{b}{x^2} f_a f_b \left(1 - \frac{1}{\sigma}\right)$$

$$= \frac{b}{x^2} f_a f_b \left(\frac{\sigma - 1}{\sigma}\right) \tag{6}$$

From (6), the relative share of a factor increases as its quantity increases if the elasticity of substitution exceeds unity, is constant if the elasticity of substitution is unity, and falls as its quantity increases if the elasticity of substitution is less than unity. Correspondingly, the relative share of a factor increases, is constant, or decreases when the quantity of the other factor increases, according as the elasticity of substitution is less than, equal to, or greater than unity.

Technical progress can be considered as increasing the effective quantities of the factors. If the effective quantity of a increases at the same rate as that of b, progress is 'neutral', in the sense that the marginal products of natural units of the factors increase at the same rate; if the effective quantity of a increases faster than that of b, technical progress is 'a-saving', or biased against a; and conversely.

To deal with the general case, let

$$\frac{1}{a} \frac{da}{dt}, = \beta \frac{1}{b} \frac{db}{dt} = \beta \lambda,$$

where λ is the proportional rate of increase per time period in the effective quantity of b due to technical progress, and β is a coefficient reflecting the bias of technical progress (a-saving or b-saving according to whether β is greater or less than unity).

$$\frac{dK_a}{dt} = f_a \frac{da}{dt} + a f_{aa} \frac{da}{dt} + a f_{ab} \frac{db}{dt}$$

$$= \lambda (a f_a \beta + a^2 f_{aa} \beta + a b f_{ab})$$

$$= \lambda (a f_a \beta - a b f_{ab} \beta + a b f_{ab})$$

89

$$= \lambda a f_a\left(\beta - \frac{b f_b f_{ab}}{f_a f_b}(\beta-1)\right)$$

$$= \lambda K_a\left(\frac{\beta\sigma - k_b(\beta-1)}{\sigma}\right) \tag{7}$$

Progress can (quite obviously) only reduce a factor's absolute share if it is biased towards saving that factor.

The necessary condition for a reduction in the absolute share is

$$\beta\sigma < k_b(\beta-1)$$

or

$$(k_b - \sigma)\beta > k_b \tag{8}$$

which requires that both $\beta > 1$ and $\sigma < k_b$. Note that the latter necessary condition is the same as the necessary and sufficient condition previously established for an increase in the quantity of a factor to reduce its absolute share.

$$\frac{dk_a}{dt} = \frac{1}{x^2}\left[bf_b\left(f_a\frac{da}{dt} + af_{aa}\frac{da}{dt} + af_{ab}\frac{db}{dt}\right)\right.$$

$$\left. - af_a\left(f_b\frac{db}{dt} + bf_{bb}\frac{db}{dt} + bf_{ab}\frac{da}{dt}\right)\right]$$

$$= \frac{1}{x^2}\left[bf_b(af_a\beta\lambda + a^2 f_{aa}\beta\lambda + abf_{ab}\lambda)\right.$$

$$\left. - af_a(bf_b\lambda + b^2 f_{bb}\lambda + abf_{ab}\beta\lambda)\right]$$

$$= \frac{1}{x^2}\left[bf_b(af_a\beta\lambda - abf_{ab}\beta\lambda + abf_{ab}\lambda)\right.$$

$$\left. - af_a(bf_b\lambda - abf_{ab}\lambda + abf_{ab}\beta\lambda)\right]$$

$$= \frac{1}{x^2}af_abf_b\left[\beta\lambda - \lambda - (af_a + bf_b)\frac{f_{ab}}{f_a f_b}\beta\lambda + (af_a + bf_b)\frac{f_{ab}}{f_a f_b}\lambda\right]$$

$$= k_a k_b (\beta\lambda - \lambda)\left(1 - \frac{1}{\sigma}\right)$$

$$= k_a k_b (\beta\lambda - \lambda)\frac{\sigma - 1}{\sigma} \tag{9}$$

Technical progress leaves the relative shares unchanged if either the progress is 'neutral', or the elasticity of substitution is unity. If progress is biased against a factor and the elasticity of substitution differs from unity, the factor's relative share rises or falls according as the elasticity of substitution exceeds or falls short of unity.

These results are of course obvious from the previous results for increases in factor quantities and the formulation of technical progress in terms of increases in effective factor quantities.

(b) The One-Sector Growth Model

(i) Convergence on the Equilibrium Path

For the purpose of constructing the one-sector growth model, we specify the production function of the previous sections as

$$X = h(K,L)$$

where X is output and K and L represent capital and labour respectively. Making use of the constant returns to scale assumption, the production function is more conveniently specified as

$$X = Lf\left(\frac{K}{L}\right) \tag{10}$$

To introduce growth, the labour force is assumed to grow at a constant exponential rate $n = 1/L.dL/dt$, as a result of either natural increase or 'Harrod-neutral' technical progress or both. Capital is assumed to grow according to the assumption that a constant proportion of the output of the economy is saved, i.e.

91

$$k = \frac{1}{K}\frac{dK}{dt} = \frac{sX}{K} \qquad (11)$$

(Note that this assumes that capital lasts for ever.)

Total differentiation of (10) with respect to time yields an equation for the growth rate of output

$$x = \frac{1}{X}\frac{dX}{dt} = n + \frac{Kf'}{X}(k-n)$$

$$= \mu_L n + \mu_K k \qquad (12)$$

where $\mu_K = Kf'/X$ is capital's share in output, and $\mu_L = 1 - \mu_K$ is labour's share in output.

Differentiating (11),

$$\frac{dk}{dt} = \frac{sX}{K}(x-k) \qquad (13)$$

Hence if $x > k$, k will rise, and if $x < k$, k will fall over time. Further, from (12), $dx/dk = \mu_K < 1$, so that an increase in k when k is less than x will raise k towards x, and a decrease in k when k is greater than x will lower towards x. Therefore, k must converge on x. Substituting $k = x$ in (12) yields the result

$$k = x = n \qquad (14)$$

That is, in the long run the rates of growth of output and capital stock will converge on the exogenously given rate of growth of the labour force. In this situation it may be noted $n = sX/K$, the left-hand side of which is Harrod's 'natural' rate of growth and the right-hand side of which is his 'warranted' rate of growth, the savings ratio divided by the capital-output ratio (R. F. Harrod, *Towards a Dynamic Economics*).

The foregoing model assumes that capital lasts for ever; however, depreciation can be introduced and shown to make no difference if depreciation is assumed to occur as a constant proportion of the capital stock. For on this assumption

92

$$k = \frac{sX}{K} - \delta \qquad (15)$$

where δ is the proportional rate of depreciation, and disappears on differentiation to yield the same equation (13).

The model also assumes that accumulation of capital is governed by a single aggregate savings ratio. It is more usual, and more interesting, to assume that capital and labour have different savings ratios, capital's savings ratio being higher than labour's. As mentioned in the text, this suggests the possibility of redistribution of income towards capital in the process of accumulation (which would occur with an elasticity of substitution greater than unity) producing an unstable equilibrium and therefore multiple growth equilibria. That this is not so can be proven quite simply. Two proofs are provided here, both involving the property that in growth equilibrium savings must be just sufficient to keep capital per head intact as the labour force grows.

For both proofs, it is convenient to rewrite the production function in per capita terms (bars over symbols denoting division by the labour force):

$$\bar{X} = f(\bar{K}) \qquad (16)$$

The first proof, due to Robert M. Solow (see my *Essays in Monetary Economics*, p. 149, n. 1), depends on the fact that the investment per unit of capital required to keep capital intact is constant, and proves that saving per unit of capital falls as capital per head increases. The overall savings ratio is a weighted average of the two factor savings ratios s_K and s_L:

$$s = s_L \frac{\bar{X} - f'\bar{K}}{\bar{X}} + s_K \frac{f'\bar{K}}{\bar{X}} = s_L + (s_K - s_L)\frac{f'\bar{K}}{\bar{X}} \qquad (17)$$

and $\qquad \dfrac{s\bar{X}}{\bar{K}} = s_L \dfrac{\bar{X}}{\bar{K}} + (s_K - s_L)f' \qquad (18)$

As $\overline{K}$ increases, both the average product $(\overline{X}/\overline{K})$ and the marginal product (f') of capital must fall, and therefore so must savings per unit of capital.

The second proof shows that growth equilibrium must be stable. Define net savings per capita as the excess of savings per capita over the amount required to keep capital per head constant:

$$s' = s_L\overline{X}+(s_K-s_L)\overline{K}f'-n\overline{K} \tag{19}$$

$$\frac{\delta s'}{\delta \overline{K}} = s_Lf'+(s_K-s_L)(f'+\overline{K}f'')-n \tag{20}$$

In growth equilibrium s' must be zero. Setting s' equal to zero in (19) and substituting the resulting expression for n in (20), in the neighbourhood of growth equilibrium

$$\frac{\delta s'}{\delta \overline{K}} = s_L\left(f'-\frac{\overline{X}}{\overline{K}}\right)+(s_K-s_L)\overline{K}f'' \tag{21}$$

Since the marginal product of capital must be less than the average product $(f'<\overline{X}/\overline{K})$ and the marginal product of capital must be diminishing $(f''<0)$ the right-hand side must be negative and $\delta s'/\delta \overline{K}<0$. The economy must decumulate capital per head if capital per head is above the equilibrium level, and conversely, so that growth equilibrium must be stable; and this rules out the possibility of multiple growth equilibrium.

(ii) The 'Golden Rule' of Accumulation

Since in the long run the economy converges on a growth rate determined by the exogenously given growth rate of the labour force, questions about the influence of the economy's savings behaviour on its growth rate are pointless, except with respect to the period of transition to a new equilibrium growth path, in which case the answer is obvious. Instead, interest centres on the influence of the overall savings ratio on consumption per head along the equilibrium growth path (the difference between output per head and the investment required to keep capital intact), and specifically on the savings ratio that will maximize consumption per head. The mathematical problem is to maximize

$$\bar{C} = (1-s)\bar{X} \tag{22}$$

with respect to the savings ratio, s.

First note that $\bar{X} = f(\bar{K})$ can be written

$$\bar{X} = f\left(\frac{K}{X} \cdot \bar{X}\right) \tag{23}$$

Differentiating,

$$d\bar{X} = f'\left(\frac{K}{X} d\bar{X} + \bar{X}d\left(\frac{K}{X}\right)\right)$$

$$= \frac{f'\bar{X}d\left(\frac{K}{X}\right)}{1 - f'\dfrac{K}{X}}$$

$$= \frac{f'\bar{X}d\left(\frac{K}{X}\right)}{1 - \mu_K} \tag{24}$$

Also, treating $x = k = n$ as constants, and using equation (11) ($sX/K = k$),

$$\frac{d\left(\frac{K}{X}\right)}{ds} = \frac{1}{k} = \frac{K}{sX} \tag{25}$$

Hence, substituting (25) into (24)

$$\frac{\delta\bar{X}}{\delta s} = \frac{f'\bar{K}}{(1-\mu_K)s} \tag{26}$$

Finally, differentiating (22) with respect to s,

$$\frac{\delta \bar{C}}{\delta s} = \bar{X}\left(-1+\frac{1-s}{1-\mu_K}\frac{f'K}{s\bar{X}}\right)$$

$$= \bar{X}\left(-1+\frac{1-s}{1-\mu_K}\frac{\mu_K}{s}\right)$$

$$= \bar{X}\left(\frac{\mu_K-s}{s(1-\mu_K)}\right) \qquad (27)$$

Maximum consumption per head requires $s = \mu_K$, that is, that the savings ratio be equal to the share of capital in total output. By using the fact that $\mu_K = f'K/X$ and $s = nK/X$ and equating and cancelling common terms, this requirement can be expressed equivalently in the form $f' = n$, i.e. the marginal product of capital (the rate of interest) must be equal to the rate of growth of the labour force.

Note that the 'golden rule' requirement will be fulfilled if labour is assumed to consume all its income and capital is assumed to save all of its income.

A Comment on the General Equilibrium Analysis of Excise Taxes*

In a recent paper, Paul Wells has presented an attempt at a general-equilibrium analysis of excise tax incidence, for a two-person two-factor two-commodity world, employing an ingenious geometrical technique similar in some respects to those commonly employed in international trade theory.[1] Such attempts to broaden the theoretical approach to tax incidence are of course to be welcomed, and Wells has opened a promising new line of attack: but unfortunately, in constructing his geometrical model Wells has incorporated a fundamental confusion between income and output which invalidates his analysis, or at least makes it depend for its validity on a peculiarly unrealistic assumption about the way in which income is distributed in his model economy. Revision of the model in the direction of orthodoxy is, however, relatively simple: it does not alter the qualitative conclusions reached as to the factors which govern the distribution of the burdens and benefits from excise taxes between individuals, though it does lead to the conclusion that the conditions under which an individual's

* Reprinted with permission from *The American Economic Review*, XLV (March 1956), pp. 151–6.
[1] Paul Wells, 'A General Equilibrium Analysis of Excise Taxes', *American Economic Review*, XLV (June 1955) pp. 345–59. All page references in what follows are to this article.

benefit from an excise tax can outweigh its burden on him are more restrictive than Wells' analysis implies.

The fundamental confusion referred to is embodied in Wells' notion of a 'division-of-output function' (*KL* in Figure I, p. 347), which 'states the ratio in which output is divided between *A* and *B* for all possible output combinations' (p. 346) on the community transformation curve. This cannot be correct. What the function must show is the division of *income*, or command over output, when factors are rewarded at their marginal productivities for the levels of production of the two goods shown by the corresponding point on the transformation curve. Alternatively, and as Wells uses it in his subsequent analysis, the function shows the amounts of the two commodities each individual would receive if each were given a share in the total *output of each commodity* equal to the share he receives of aggregate income.

In his analysis of market equilibrium in the absence and presence of excise taxes, Wells takes the point on the division-of-output function corresponding to the production point on the transformation curve as representing the initial stocks of output held by the two individuals in the economy, and proceeds to show how they would modify these stocks through exchange in the market along familiar contract-box lines. This procedure implicitly assumes that factor owners are remunerated in *pro rata* shares of aggregate physical output; and it gives the model several peculiar features, one of which is that exchange takes place, and taxable capacity exists, only to the extent that individuals wish to consume commodities in different proportions from the community average at the same price ratio.[1]

[1] In Wells' example, the farmer is assumed to want relatively more clothing and relatively less food than the worker; clearly the reverse might be true, making the farmer a seller of clothing and buyer of food (on the argument of the model) and requiring a modification of the analysis. Further, the introduction of a tax might lead to the elimination of exchange or a reversal of trading roles, possibilities not considered by Wells. Another peculiar feature of the

Obviously, the relevance of the model depends on the appropriateness of the assumption that factor owners are rewarded by the transfer to them of *pro rata* shares of physical output. This assumption seems highly unrealistic for the type of market economy with which Wells is concerned, in which production and exchange are separated;[1] it would be more reasonable to assume that factor owners are remunerated in generalized purchasing power, which they are free to spend as they like on commodities purchased from the production sector, and that excise taxes are levied on all such purchases of the taxed good.

In terms of Wells' geometrical construction, the division of income between the two individuals would be represented, not by a point on the division-of-output function, but by a line through that point having the same slope as the marginal rate of transformation, which would indicate the combinations of goods the individuals could purchase (at factor cost) with their incomes from factor ownership. Equilibrium in the absence of taxes would be determined, as in Wells' construction, by the tangency of indifference curves of the two individuals with this

model, emerging from the assumptions mentioned above, is that the Paretian optimum conditions are violated for one individual only (p. 353; Wells actually says 'for at least one individual' but his analysis provides no basis for the insertion of the phrase 'at least').

[1] The assumption might be made that factors are remunerated in kind and allocated to industries so that the proportions of *A*-owned to *B*-owned factors are the same in both industries – an allocation which could be justified by chance considerations. This would ensure each owner a *pro rata* share of physical output to hold or exchange; but the introduction of a tax would then give factor owners the incentive to evade taxes by reallocating factors to industries in accord with their demands for final output. A possible alternative assumption, that the productive sector has two parts, one of which uses *A*'s factors and turns over their output to him, and the other of which uses *B*'s factors and surrenders its output to him, would not lead to *pro rata* shares in physical output, since the two sectors would have different comparative advantages and be led to specialize partially or completely in food and clothing respectively. This assumption would also give rise to tax evasion through the productive sector, since taxation would give an incentive to factor owners to charge different prices for the same factor to the different productive sectors.

line at the same point on it. But the introduction of a tax on a particular commodity would be represented, not by a different line from the division-of-output point, but by two lines, one for each individual, starting from the intercepts of the income-division-line with the two sides of the contract box representing the untaxed commodity; and equilibrium individual consumption with excise taxation would be represented by tangencies of individual indifference curves with these lines.

The construction is illustrated in Figure I, which represents a position of general equilibrium with excise taxation on clothing. In the diagram, PP' is the social transformation curve between food and clothing, and P_t is the equilibrium social production point. D is Wells' division-of-output point, and MM' (with slope equal to the marginal rate of transformation at P_t) is the income-division line. With social production P_t, individual A receives an income equal in value, measured at factor cost, to any combination of goods along MM' (referred to the origin O). With this income he could purchase OM of food, the untaxed good; but his purchases of clothing are subject to the excise tax, and so the consumption possibilities open to him are represented by the consumption-possibility line MN rather than by MM', the difference in slope between the two lines corresponding to the difference between the market price and factor cost of clothing as determined by the rate of the tax. His equilibrium consumption combination, shown by the consumption point P_a, is determined by the tangency of one of his indifference curves (I_a) with his consumption-possibility line MN. Similarly, B's income is shown by MM' (referred to the origin P_t) but his consumption possibilities are shown by the consumption possibility line $M'N'$ and his equilibrium consumption point P_b is determined by the tangency of one of his indifference curves (I_b) with his consumption-possibility line. The gap between the two individuals' consumption points, representing P_aQ of food and QP_b of clothing, corresponds to the amounts of the two goods consumed by the taxing authority.[1] The tax has two apparent effects on welfare: besides the extraction of the tax proceeds from personal consumption, it violates the Paretian optimum condition of equality between the marginal rates of transformation in production and substitution in consumption.[2]

A third possible effect of the tax is a shift in the distribution of income brought about by a shift of demand and production from one good to the other. This shift, and the resulting 'benefit' to one of the factor owners, may go either way, depending on whether or not the reduction in consumer demand resulting from the imposition of the tax is or is not offset by the increased governmental demand for the taxed commodity.[3] The point may be illustrated by reference to Figure I. If the tax on clothing were removed, consumers' demands for goods would be shown by tangency of their indifference curves with the income-division line. If the tangency point for A lay to the left of that for B, there would be an excess demand for food at current prices, and food prices and production would have to increase to restore equilibrium; this would imply an increase in the relative income share of individual A, who is assumed to own relatively more of the factor (land) used relatively more in food production. Conversely, if the tangency point for A lay to the right of that for B, there would be an excess demand for clothing which

[1] The construction can easily be extended to deal with the case of excise taxes levied on both goods, or of any kind of income tax. It should perhaps be emphasized that the application of this technique to tax problems requires the assumption that factor supplies are completely inelastic.

[2] In contrast to the situation in Wells' model, Paretian optimum conditions remain fulfilled as between the two consumers.

[3] It is not clear whether Wells recognizes the possibility that production may actually shift towards the taxed commodity; his geometrical analysis indicates an unambiguous shift of production towards the untaxed commodity, due to his assumption that taxes are spent only on the untaxed good, but his verbal argument (p. 356) allows the possibility of a different expenditure of tax proceeds and explicitly mentions the possibility of no production change, while he emphasizes that his investigation of government demand is incomplete.

would have to be remedied by a production shift towards clothing and a corresponding increase in B's income share. More concretely, it can be shown that the imposition of a tax will require a production shift away from or towards the taxed

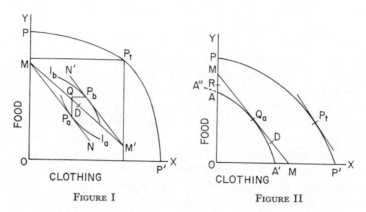

FIGURE I   FIGURE II

commodity, according to whether the elasticity of consumer demand for that commodity is greater or less than the proportion of tax proceeds spent by the government on that commodity (government expenditure being valued at factor cost).[1] On the

[1] For low tax rates, the reduction in quantity demanded by consumers is $e.t.q$, where e is the elasticity of demand, t the tax rate (as a proportion of factor cost) and q the quantity initially purchased; tax proceeds are approximately $t.q.p$, where p is the untaxed price, equal to factor cost; and the change in quantity demanded is $(cp-e)tq$, where c is the physical quantity of the taxed good purchased by the government when its tax income increases by one unit, and cp is the money value of this quantity, or the proportion of an increment of tax proceeds which is spent on the taxed good, value and expenditure being measured at factor cost. The quantity demanded increases or decreases according to whether cp is greater or less than e; the economic meaning of this is stated in the text. A more accurate formula for the proceeds of the tax, which takes account of the consequential change in consumption, is $(1-et)$ tpq.

The term cp may be interpreted as a governmental marginal propensity to spend on the taxed good. Since the consumer demand elasticity contains both a marginal propensity to spend and a positive substitution term, it follows

assumption that normally demand elasticities exceed unity and that the untaxed good is not 'inferior' in government consumption, the tax must however produce a production shift towards the untaxed commodity. The same conclusion would follow from the assumption that the government's preference for the taxed good is no stronger than that of the taxpayers.[1]

Under the 'normal' conditions defined in the preceding paragraph, the individual who owns relatively more of the factor relatively more required in the production of the untaxed good will derive an income 'benefit' from the tax, in the form of an increase in his relative income share. The possibility arises that this benefit may outweigh the burden of the tax on the individual, leaving him better off than he would be in the absence of taxation. One way of expressing this proposition is to state that the increase in income may more than offset the increase in the price he pays for the taxed commodity. But this statement is misleading: it can be shown that, for a certain range of production shift, the benefit can only outweigh the burden if the effect of the tax is to reduce the market price of the taxed good (including the tax) below what it would be in the absence of the tax.

To pursue the analysis of this problem, it is necessary to investigate the behaviour of the income-division line as production shifts towards food and away from clothing. This can be done rather simply, by drawing on the factor-price-equalization literature, and specifically on the proposition that in a two-country two-factor two-commodity free-trade world, with linear homogeneous production functions the same for each

that a necessary condition for demand for the taxed commodity to increase is that the government have a stronger preference for (higher marginal propensity to spend on) the taxed good than does the tax-paying community.

[1] The problem dealt with in this paragraph, and the analysis of it, exactly parallel a familiar problem in international trade theory, namely the conditions under which the imposition of a tariff turns a country's terms of trade against it.

commodity in the two countries and characterized by the property that a commodity which makes relatively intensive use of a factor at one factor-price ratio does so at all factor-price ratios, absolute factor prices will be equalized as long as both countries continue to produce both commodities, even though factors are immobile between countries.[1] Reversing the argument for the present problem, the income obtained by a factor owner, and his share in total income, under different patterns of aggregate production, can be determined from the transformation curve for the factors he himself owns, because his income would be no different if his factors could be combined only with each other, and their products sold, than if the factors themselves were sold freely and combined with factors owned by the other member of the community. The equivalence holds strictly only for patterns of aggregate production and commodity prices making it profitable to employ this set of factors in producing both goods; but the principle can be extended to take care of cases falling outside this restriction.

The procedure is illustrated in Figure II, where PP' represents, as before, the social transformation curve, and AA' is the transformation curve for A's factors only. For the aggregate production point P_t, A's income would be the same as if his factors were employed in producing at the production point Q_a (the point at which A's marginal rate of transformation between products would be the same as B's and the community's); the income-division line would be MM' and Wells' division-of-output point would be at D.

For shifts of aggregate production towards food, up to the point at which the marginal social rate of transformation became equal to the slope of AA' at A, the income-division line

[1] See P. A. Samuelson, 'International Trade and the Equalization of Factor Prices', *Economic Journal*, LVIII (June 1948), pp. 163–84 and 'International Factor Price Equalization Once Again', *ibid.*, LIX (June 1949), pp. 181–92; also I. F. Pearce, 'The Factor Price Equalization Myth', *Review of Economic Studies*, 1951–52, XIX(2), pp. 111–23.

would rotate around AA', and its intercept with the Y-axis would move towards the point A. From this it follows that individual A could only be made better off by a tax-induced shift of production towards food if the shift, and the accompanying reduction in the relative marginal cost of clothing production, went far enough to make the new tax-inclusive price of clothing lower than the old tax-free price. For suppose the tax shifts production so that the income-division line intercepts the Y-axis at R instead of M; A's consumption possibilities will now be shown by a consumption-possibility line through R, reflecting market prices including the tax, and it would only be possible for A to reach a higher indifference curve along this line than he did along the old income-division line if the new line intersected the old – which would require that the new market price of clothing, including the tax, be lower than the former tax-free price.[1]

The point A corresponds to complete specialization of A's resources on food production; alternatively, it is defined by the condition that factor prices are such that maximum-profit food production employs factors in the same ratio as A happens to own them. With a further shift of production towards food, the consequential variation in relative factor prices would make it profitable to hire additional labour from B to co-operate with A's land in producing food. This could be represented by a continuation of the AA' curve to the left of the Y-axis (AA'' in Figure II), the cost of the hired labour appearing as negative clothing production by A. The income-division line would be determined by a tangency as before, and A's net income measured in food would be given by the intercept of the income-division line with the Y-axis. But the tangency point would now lie to the left of the Y-axis, and shifts of production towards food would now increase A's income measured in food; hence it

[1] This is of course only a necessary, not a sufficient, condition for A to benefit on balance from the tax.

would now be possible for the tax to make A better off on balance, even though the market price of clothing had been increased by the tax.

To summarize: for tax-induced shifts in production which leave the profitable land-to-labour ratio in food production higher than the ratio of land-to-labour possessed by A, the tax can only benefit A on balance if its effect is to reduce the market price (including tax) of clothing: for shifts which make the profitable land-to-labour ratio in food production lower than the ratio of land-to-labour possessed by A, the tax may benefit A on balance even though it raises the market price of clothing. These results underline the crucial importance of differences in asset-holdings as between individuals to the theory of tax incidence. They also suggest the need for an investigation of the conditions which would permit a tax to reduce the market price of the taxed good, an investigation which cannot be pursued here.

A Geometrical Note on General Equilibrium with Public Goods

The standard two-commodity two-factor model used in the theory of international trade to represent the domestic economy (the Heckscher-Ohlin-Samuelson model) provides the simplest possible representation of the interaction of technology, factor supplies, and individual preferences in the determination of general equilibrium in production, consumption, commodity and factor prices, and the distribution of income. That model typically assumes that the commodities produced are private goods. It can, however, readily be extended to the analysis of the case of public goods, a case in which theorists on public finance problems have been increasingly interested. This is the purpose of this note.

(a) *The Case of Two Private Goods*

Figure I shows the transformation curve for the economy (TT'), derived from the economy's fixed endowment of the two factors and the production functions for the two commodities, assumed to be subject to constant returns to scale and to use the two factors with relatively different intensities at any realizable relative factor-price ratio. The slope of the transformation curve at any point such as P_0 is the marginal rate of transformation of one good into the other, or commodity-price ratio for the corresponding combination of goods produced, whose value (the national income) is represented by the budget line MM'. According to the Stolper-Samuelson relation, to each commodity-price ratio there corresponds a unique relative factor-price ratio and unique marginal products of each factor in each industry, the relationship between the commodity-price ratio and factor-price ratio being such that as the relative price of a commodity rises and production shifts towards producing more of it, the marginal productivity in terms of both goods of the factor used relatively intensively in producing that commodity rises and the marginal productivity in terms of both goods of the other factor falls, the relative factor-price ratio changing in favour of the factor used relatively intensively in producing the goods whose relative price has risen.

The problem of income distribution can be introduced by assuming that ownership of the two factors with which the country is endowed is divided somehow among two individuals, 1 and 2. If individual 1 has a relatively large share of the factor used relatively intensively in producing commodity X, his share in the total income of the community will rise as production shifts towards X, and that of individual 2 will fall. The incomes received by the two individuals, for any production point such as P_0, are shown on the diagram by the intersections of the ray OP_0 with the income-distribution curves W_1W_1' and W_2W_2'; lines through these intersections parallel to MM' (M_1M_1' and M_2M_2') constitute the budget lines for the two individuals. Tangency of one of the indifference curves representing the preference system of the relevant individual with his budget line gives his utility-maximizing consumption point (respectively C_{10} and C_{20}). Vector addition of these consumption bundles (completion of the parallelogram of which two sides are OC_{10} and OC_{20}) gives the total consumption demand for the community as a whole, C_0.

As the diagram is drawn, C_0 coincides exactly with P_0, so that the economy is in full general equilibrium. If C_0 lay north-west of P_0 on MM', there would be an excess demand for Y and excess supply of X, production would have to shift towards Y, with a fall in the relative price of X and a redistribution of income from individual 1 towards individual 2. Conversely, if C_0 lay south-east of P_0 on MM', there would be an excess supply of Y and demand for X, and a shift of production towards X and income distribution towards individual 1.

In the model as presented, the redistribution of income involved in a shift in the production point P_0 is a redistribution of purchasing power. However, even if each individual had the same proportional ownership of each factor of production, a redistribution of real income would occur if the individuals preferred to consume the two goods in different ratios at the same commodity-price ratio, because one would be a net supplier and the other a net demander of each good, so that a price ratio change would have a positive income effect on the one and negative income effect on the other. This income redistribution effect, whether mediated through differences in relative factor ownership or differences in preferences, or both, makes the effect of a commodity price change on excess demand for a commodity ambiguous, even when both goods are assumed to be 'normal' (non-inferior) in each person's consumption, and introduces the possibility of unstable equilibrium. Specifically, while the transformation effect in production and the substitution effect in consumption of an increase in the relative price of one of the commodities must operate to reduce the excess demand for it, the redistribution effect may operate to increase the excess demand for it, perhaps sufficiently strongly to overcome the other two effects, and produce a net increase in excess demand as the price rises.

Where differences in relative factor ownership dominate over differences in preferences, the necessary but not sufficient condition for this effect is that each individual has a relative marginal preference for the good that uses relatively intensively the factor in which he has a relatively large ownership share, in the sense that when his income rises he increases his consumption of that good relatively more than the other individual would do. Concretely in terms of Figure I, individual 1 must have a marginal preference for X and individual 2 for Y (i.e. the income-expansion line of individual 1 must be flatter than that of individual 2). Where individuals have the same relative shares in ownership of the factors, the marginal propensities to consume must be inversely related to the average propensities. In terms of Figure I, if the income distribution curves for the two individuals were identical in shape, the income expansion line for individual 2 through C_{20} must be flatter than that of individual 1 through C_{10}. (It should be noted that as the diagram is drawn a rise in the relative price of X (fall in the relative price of Y) redistributes income towards individual 1 as a relatively large owner of the factor used intensively in producing X, and towards individual 2 as a relatively heavy consumer of Y, hence the two necessary conditions produce opposite requirements on the income-expansion lines.)

Where an increase in the price of a commodity at an equilibrium production and consumption point increases the excess demand for it, that equilibrium point will be unstable. But so long as it is assumed that at least one individual always demands some of both goods, there will always exist a stable equilibrium point, involving positive production of both goods, on each side of the unstable point along the transformation curve.

(b) *One Private, one Public Good*

A pure public good is one for which enjoyment by one individual does not in any degree exclude enjoyment by the other. Hence, in contrast to private goods, where each individual has to pay the cost of production of what he consumes, the cost of a public good can be shared among the individuals enjoying it, and the problem of optimization is to achieve the scale of production of the public good, on a shared cost basis, that maximizes the social welfare (in the Pareto-optimal sense).

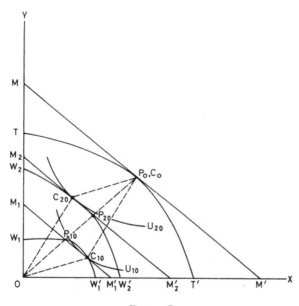

FIGURE I

To deal with the case in which one of the two goods is a public good, assume that commodity Y in Figure I is the public good (in Figure II). Then Y_0 is the amount of that good available for each individual to consume. But if individual 1 had to pay the full cost of production of the public good, he would demand only Y_{10} of it, while if individual 2 had to pay the full cost of production of it, he would demand only Y_{20}. The cost could,

III

however, be shared, and if neither had to pay the full cost it would be possible for some cost-sharing arrangement to permit the amount Y_0 to be demanded. To determine this, rotate the budget lines $M_1 M_1'$ and $M_2 M_2'$ rightward about M_1' and M_2' respectively, tracing out the demand curves of the two individuals

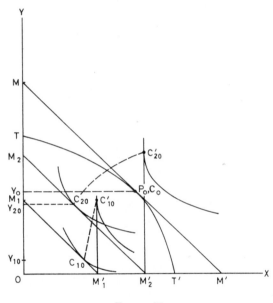

FIGURE II

for the public good as its price to them falls from cost of production to zero. The corresponding consumption points are C_{10}' and C_{20}'. If either of these points falls below the horizontal line $Y_0 P_0$, as is the case with C_{10}' in Figure II, it is evident that no feasible cost-sharing arrangement exists that would permit P_0 to be an equilibrium consumption point. If, on the other hand,

112

both points lie above the line Y_0P_0, such an arrangement may exist.

This possibility is illustrated in Figure III. To determine whether P_0 is a feasible equilibrium, consider the points C_1 and C_2 at which the two demand curves cross the horizontal line

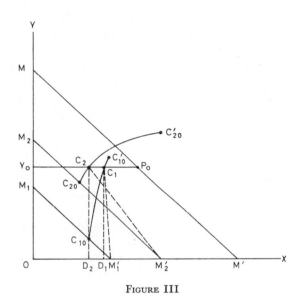

FIGURE III

Y_0P_0, to each of which corresponds a price ratio, represented by the slopes respectively of C_1M_1' and C_2M_2'. If the average of these slopes is exactly double the slope of the budget line MM^1, P_0 will be a position of general equilibrium; if it is more than double, the two individuals together will be unwilling to pay the total cost of Y_0, and production will have to shift towards more of X and less of Y; conversely, if the average is less than double the slope of the budget line, the two individuals together would

H   113 be willing to pay more than the cost of production of Y_0, and production would have to shift towards more of Y and less of X.

The critical condition determining whether there is excess supply of or excess demand for Y can be represented diagrammatically as follows. Drop perpendiculars from C_1 and C_2 to D_1 and D_2 on the X-axis; mark off D_3 such that $M_1'D_3 = D_2M_2'$; draw a line joining C_1 and D_3. If C_1D_3 is steeper than the budget line, the total amount that the two individuals will pay for Y_0 is less than its cost in terms of X, and vice versa. (The second possibility is illustrated in Figure III.)

As in the case of two private goods, the general equilibrium in this case is not necessarily unique, that is, there is a possibility of an unstable equilibrium position bounded by two stable equilibrium positions (more generally, of an odd number of alternatively stable and unstable equilibria). This possibility arises because a shift of the production point along the transformation curve redistributes earned income towards the individual who owns relatively more of the factor used relatively intensively in producing the good whose production has increased; if that individual has a relative marginal preference for the commodity towards which production has shifted, the increase in demand for it due to income redistribution may outweigh the adverse substitution effect and the increase in output of it. More precisely in the context of a public good, on the assumption previously made that individual 2 owns relatively more of the factor used intensively in producing the public good, an increase in production of that good will increase his income, and if he has a relatively strong marginal preference for the public good as compared with individual 1, he may be willing to assume a larger share of the cost of the public good in order to induce individual 1 to agree to a larger quantity of it being produced.

The foregoing analysis has assumed that the two individuals in the economy co-operate honestly in revealing their preferences as regards the public good. As is well known, there are generally incentives for concealment of preferences, because one individual might be able to increase his welfare by inveigling the other into assuming a larger share of the cost of a smaller output of public goods. This possibility is illustrated in Figure IV, where

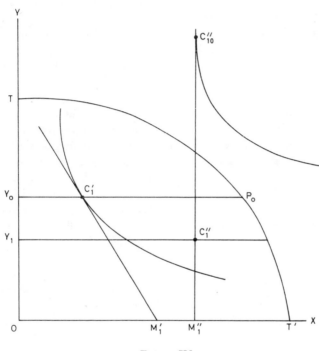

FIGURE IV

C_1' represents an equilibrium position reached on a basis of cost-sharing, and C_1'' represents the equilibrium that would be reached if individual 1 refused to pay any of the costs of producing the public good. Y_1, the amount of the public good that individual 2 would pay for if he had to pay the full cost, is far short of the amount Y_2 that individual 1 would like to have available at a zero price to him; but free consumption of that amount of the public good, together with expenditure of all his earned income on the private good, makes individual 1 better off than if he shared the cost of production of Y_1 of the public good with individual 2 and thereby fulfilled the marginal conditions for a Pareto optimum.

Figure IV implicitly brings out a fairly obvious but interesting point. By refusing to share the costs of the public good, and so reducing the amount of it produced, individual 1 shifts production towards X, which uses relatively intensively the factor of which he owns a relatively large share, and so increases his own earned income. Conversely, individual 2 would gain in earned income if production shifted the other way. Thus, over and above the consideration just mentioned that an individual with a given income may gain on balance by reducing his cost share at the expense of reducing the amount of the public good available, the individual may also gain directly in earned income by a reduction in the output of the public good. This point is of course a familiar one in the politics of public works.

Two Public Goods
The case of two public goods is a complex one, since the earned incomes of the two individuals in this case place no restrictions on the welfare levels they can achieve, these depending instead on the allocation of the community's total resources between production of the two goods. A Pareto-optimal solution is possible only if the two individuals have identical preference systems, and hence agree on the allocation of resources; in this case, the solution is depicted by the tangency with the transformation curve of an indifference curve belonging to the common preference system. If, as is more interesting to assume,

preferences differ, different allocations would be optimal for the two individuals, and there is no obvious mechanism for resolving the difference. The case is depicted in Figure V, where P_1 is the production pattern that would maximize the welfare of individual 1, and P_2 is the production pattern that

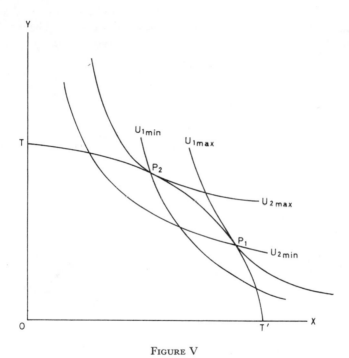

FIGURE V

would maximize the welfare of individual 2. The indifference curves corresponding to welfare maximization for the respective individuals are marked U_1 max and U_2 max respectively; the indifference curves for the other individual at the maximization point are marked U_2 min and U_1 min respectively, because it is obvious that it would always pay both individuals to move from any point on the transformation curve in the ranges TP_1 and TP_2 to P_1 and P_2 respectively. The production point chosen must obviously lie within the range on the transformation curve P_1P_2 inclusive. But where it will lie cannot be determined, as in the previous case, by a process of marginal adjustment and maximization subject to a budget constraint, for the budget constraint for each is the social transformation curve. There is a direct conflict of interest, which has to be resolved by some mechanism not contained in the model.